FRAGMENTS

Ian Okell

A book about beliefs, doubts and miracles
- and some reasons to stand up and be counted

Published in 2015 by FeedARead.com Publishing
Copyright © Ian Okell

A CIP catalogue record for this title is available from the British Library.

'The Gods of the Copybook Headings'

*'As sure as water will wet us,
as surely as fire will burn . . .'*

Rudyard Kipling

Cover: Ian Okell

Index

Preface

How this book came about

Following the publication of my recent book, 'Barabbas', a fictional autobiography of that character, I had wanted to write a similar version of the Judas story. But whereas the life story of Barabbas was a blank canvas, which I could fill in as I pleased, the same couldn't be said for Judas. There were altogether too many witnesses to the surrounding events to allow me the fictional freedom to develop his life in way that I felt necessary for a novel. Somehow I couldn't get myself into the story in a way that I was comfortable with.

Eventually, I decided to treat his story as a piece of non fiction, a documentary report with my associated comments and views, even if the result was too short to be published as a book. The fact is that I was principally interested in trying to set out the story to my own satisfaction, and wasn't all that bothered about whether or not it ever appeared in print.

With that in mind, I began to assemble my research notes for what was probably going to be no more than a long essay on the improbability of the Judas story, as reported in the New Testament.

My book on Barabbas contains something like 100,000 words, and my research notes for it, folders full of rough scribbles with multiple crossings out, asterisks and under linings, were probably longer than that. My routine, which I imagine to be common to many writers, is to undertake a mountain of research and then allow that to inform or influence the final text, but never simply to quote it verbatim. Thus, in some places, for example, five pages of research notes may provide the background and justification for one page of finished text. I don't regard this as hard work, one of the reasons that I enjoy writing is that I enjoy the research.

Fact finding trips (research on the hoof) for the adventures I write, have included Margaret and I spending day after sunny day driving slowly round Chesapeake Bay in Virginia, exploring old airfields in eastern France, tracing the route of Victorian railway tracks on the north Yorkshire moors, following Fagin's footsteps round old London docks and warehouses, and learning to fly a Second World War Fieseler Storch aircraft. Our most recent outing was finding out how to load nuclear warheads onto a London Underground train. You could scarcely call it hard work, it's the most fun I've ever had. You can see why I prefer it to my day job.

Admittedly the research for this particular book required me to go no further than my own study desk, but it still took me down a huge number of fascinating side turnings, areas that I would otherwise have had no reason ever to think of. It's rather like going to look something up in a dictionary and being side tracked by other words you spot on the way.

So it was, that when I found the research notes straying into areas that weren't strictly required for the proposed work, for example justifying why I was a suitable person to tell the story, I was neither troubled nor surprised. That was just my normal disorganised approach.

What did come as a surprise was that by the time I had reached around 25,000 words of supposed research, I discovered that, without realising it, I was no longer writing background notes, I was writing the book itself.

My random notes had formed themselves into a sequence of linked essays, and I hope you won't feel cheated if I leave them together and call the result a book. I'm not sure how the transition occurred, but by the time I woke up to what was going on, it had already happened. You might think I would pay more attention.

This was never planned as an autobiography, I'm not a pop singer, a professional footballer or a celebrity chef, so there's no captive market waiting to hear about my love life and early years. However, once it became clear that the only way I could make the book work was as a piece of factual description, rather than a novel, I felt it necessary to provide some details of my own background, to at least try and answer your perfectly natural question,

'Why should anyone pay the slightest attention to a low grade scribbler like you?'

This is why, while the resulting book contains some elements of my own life story, those elements have been selected to offer some sort of answer to that question, and because of their relevance to the subject. Although it's true, there are one or two diversions, where it looked as though they might be interesting enough to add to the mix. The chapter headings listed at the front of the book give you a pretty clear idea of where this leads.

I've written other books, but this is my first non fiction book, and I've taken the implicit requirement in that description very literally. And so, apart from changing the names, for obvious reasons, of people who might not wish to be associated with this public description of certain episodes, all the other details are accurate.

What follows is far more intensely personal than I had ever intended, and covers a much wider range than a simple account of my problems with the betrayal narrative. It's true that Judas and some of my other New Testament doubts are still here, but they are no longer centre stage.

The finished book seems to have expanded into more of an exploration of who I am and why I hold the beliefs I do, which, as an essentially private person, was never my intention. But when you start pulling at one end of the thread you can never be sure where it will lead.

CHAPTER ONE

The Basis of My Approach

The fact that I approach the scriptures as a run of the mill, though moderately well read believer; rather than as a trained theologian, is a two edged sword. True, I come without the benefit of a disciplined academic mind, which might have helped me sift conflicting evidence more easily, but perhaps I also come with fewer of other people's preconceptions.

Wherever my views coincide with current academic consensus it is more likely to be by chance than design. I would never claim this to be a superior position, I simply observe that it is my position.

My status as a scriptural amateur can be further confirmed by the fact that I take so much of the New Testament seriously, and in some cases literally. I tend to assume that if the New Testament says that Jesus did this, then without compelling grounds for doubt, I accept that that is probably what he did. There are a few problem areas for me, some of which are covered in this book, nonetheless that is my most usual starting point.

A routine stumbling block for a rational, or supposedly serious, approach to Christianity is the existence of miracles in the New Testament. For some people these are an embarrassment to be quietly swept aside, for others the cause of outright rejection of the whole story. My own position is somewhat different, I'm too interested and too curious to be so dismissive.

The academic approach is often not so much to explain the miraculous, as to explain it away. A good example of this is the story of Jesus walking on the stormy waters of the Sea of Galilee. An explanation that I have heard more than once from the pulpit is that this is not meant to be taken literally, and is just another parable; with the disturbed water representing disturbed and expectant Jewish public opinion, which Jesus' teaching was able to reach across, or walk over.

Perhaps this is so, but that has never been how the story sounded to me, parables are generally told by Jesus rather than about him. One can believe it or disbelieve it, that's scarcely the issue, but I can see no reason to regard this story as anything other than a piece of straight reporting. To quote Freud, sometimes a cigar really is just a good smoke. Similar approaches are routinely made to the Virgin Birth and the Resurrection.

The whole point of Jesus' time on earth lies in the miraculous, if you don't accept that, then what do you accept? And without the miraculous, what possible point is there in Holy Communion; the body and blood of Christ? Even the Protestant symbolic approach to the elements of Communion requires at least a nod to the miraculous. Explaining difficult passages is a good thing, explaining them away is not.

One might as well look at Beethoven and say, 'He was a reasonable sort of fellow, but if you take away all that music he was nothing special.' His music was the essence of the man, what made him exceptional, and why we remember him today. If all you want from life is the mundane and the ordinary, then buy yourself a goldfish and watch that swim round in predictable circles.

No matter whether you look at Beethoven or Jesus, you are hardly looking at the mundane and the ordinary. The extent to which we can emulate them is another matter, but we really shouldn't try to explain them away because they make us feel inadequate or uncomfortable.

At what point does genius shade into miraculous? I don't know the answer to that, and don't even know if there is an answer. However, when it comes to miracles it is worth remembering that anyone shown a sufficiently surprising, previously unknown scientific advance will be unable to distinguish it from magic; for magic you can read miracle.

This isn't just a caveman being shown a mobile phone or a television, there are items, perhaps still to be invented, that would impose exactly the same level of astonishment and disbelief on you and me.

However, no simple acceptance that inexplicable and irrational events do happen is sufficient to make me uncritical or unquestioning when it comes to religious belief. I accept and support the idea that people with a religious faith should, routinely, question the validity and strength of those beliefs, should examine the central pillars of their faith. Any religion that does not permit such questioning is frightened of what the answers might be.

There is certainly a danger that rigorous questioning might destroy a casual attachment, but that just reinforces the fact that simply going through the motions of observance, as a matter of habit, is somewhat pointless. Constant niggling at an already answered question is futile, but a refusal to subject your beliefs to question is worse. The trouble lies not so much in the questioning as in a determination to prejudge the answer.

It is doing no more than stating the obvious to say that faith must always be a matter of feeling before it becomes a matter of fact. Faith that arises from proof is a misuse of the word; whatever such a thing is - it isn't faith. I would further say that as the existence of God can never be objectively proven, attempts to do so are pointless. So how then should we view biblical stories of miracles?

A fairly common view is that Jesus was no more than a well intentioned preacher who, whilst he might have had a private line to God, was unable or unwilling to manifest this in any physical manner. Others, including a surprising number of senior Anglican clerics, suggest that God could, if he'd wanted, have performed miracles through Jesus - but simply chose not to.

This is a cop out, a verbal sleight of hand. If you feel uncomfortable to have miracles as a part of your religion, and wish to claim that their inclusion is no more than a 2000 year old way of establishing a narrative point, then I think you're making a mistake. Denying the possible existence of miracles, not just in the New Testament, but in life in general, indicates a rather dull and unimaginative conformity of thought, a desire to lose yourself in the safety of the herd.

When considering the presence of the miraculous in this world, despite having once thought of myself as a bit of a smart aleck, a tedious but common fault of the self taught, I have now lived long enough to begin to realise just how much I don't know. A realisation that might profitably have occurred sooner, with a more formal education. To begin to accept, as the quote has it, that this universe is not only queerer than we know, but queerer than we *can* know.

My own view is that there are events in this world, undeniably real events, which defy rational explanation, and the one word which precisely covers that definition is – miracle. Do I believe in miracles? Yes I do; if only because I can't see how I couldn't.

CHAPTER TWO

<u>What Makes a Miracle?</u>

Simply saying that I accept the existence of miracles in this life is a very easy thing to do, but without some justification isn't worth much more than saying that I believe in truth, justice and liberty for all. So what I propose is to offer some episodes from my own life, which might explain *why* I hold this view.

Somewhat prosaically, the basis for my own belief in the reality of what you can describe either as the inexplicable, or the miraculous, is based on the accumulated experiences of my own family and social life. There haven't been any visions of God or the Virgin Mary and I've never been abducted by aliens; just the slow accretion of various events, some of which, if you try hard enough and use a little self deception, you could almost explain away as normal.

I won't list things chronologically, instead I'll start with the easy stuff, an experience probably shared by many; the display of extra sensory perception by young children. Our eldest daughter, Sarah, for a few months around the age of three, knew things about our friends and relatives for which there was no rational explanation. She would say such things as,

'I'll tell Aunty Janice about that when she comes round this afternoon.'

In that particular case, as Aunty Janice lived fifty miles away and only visited very infrequently this could hardly be guesswork. We shrugged it off, only to find that an hour later Janice rang to say that owing to whatever circumstances she was free that afternoon, and would we be at home if she and her children called round? Or that Uncle David had hurt his arm, or that a specific one of her many cousins was very upset about some named and identified problem.

There were something like ten or fifteen such instances, and these were the totality of such remarks; not just a few lucky hits that we subsequently cherry picked to show how clever our daughter was. This gift only ever applied to people she knew personally and was relatively short lived, by her fourth birthday it had disappeared. We had considered introducing her to a selection of professional jockeys, on the off chance that she might let us know the upcoming winner of the 3.30 at Chester races, but sadly we didn't move fast enough.

A slightly less common experience happened to me as a young man of about seventeen. My first serious girl friend, I'll call her Becky, and I had been going out together for about nine months and then parted. No arguments or ill will, we just decided in a strangely mature sort of way that the relationship had run its course and we would both move on.

A year later, during which time there had been no contact between us, I had the most vivid dream about walking through a garden with Becky, and was convinced that I should call her. I rang her home, where her mother told me that she no longer lived there but was some sort of live in housekeeper at a large house not far away, and gave me her number. I rang Becky immediately, there was no time for her mother to have called her first. She was unsurprised to hear from me and before I could explain myself she said,

'I thought I might hear from you after that dream last night.'

We had both experienced the same dream and walked in the same garden, I even drove round there to confirm, face to face, exactly what was being said. As a divine revelation or a glimpse of the supernatural this is pretty thin stuff, but can you honestly call shared dreams normal? I'd be interested to hear a suggestion of how such a thing might work.

To move onto something significantly weirder, it's a little more involved than the first two but stick with me, I think it's worth it. In the previous paragraph I changed Becky's name because I haven't seen her since that day and know nothing of her subsequent life, so couldn't ask permission to name her. In this case, for reasons which will become clear, I have no option but to change my friend's name because I think it would annoy him if I didn't.

Tom is someone I've known since I was in junior school, and although subsequently living some distance apart, we've been seeing each other, intermittently, ever since and still do. There isn't a lot, if anything, that we don't know about each other's lives. In the spring of 1973, the year before I got married, Tom and I decided that the two of us would take a trip in his boat, a large offshore capable motor cruiser, from Cornwall down to Brittany.

The trip was fun, seeing different places and meeting different people; through the Channel Isles and along the north Brittany coast, and then back more or less the same way. On the return leg we were held up in Guernsey by bad weather and Tom and I were in a waterfront bar in the capital, Saint Peter Port. Everything was fine until I suddenly remembered that it was Saturday night and I was supposed to be having what would have been my second date with Margaret, my future wife, in Manchester that night. I called her from the noisy bar phone and apologised, blaming the bad weather.

'Where exactly are you?'

'I'm in Guernsey, with Tom.'

'Guernsey! What on earth are you doing in Guernsey, I've just had my hair done, in Manchester - and who precisely is Tom?'

Anyway, the next day the weather had cleared so we phoned across to the UK Coastguards in Falmouth, to advise them of our details and ETA at our home port of Fowey, a standard routine for long cross channel trips before the spread of small boat ship to shore radio, or mobile phones. A couple of hours into the voyage the oil warning light on one of the two engines came on and it seemed to be overheating, we couldn't find any fault but felt that we ought to shut it down and continue on just one engine. It would take longer but we weren't stuck for time, so that was what we did.

In those days before GPS, navigation was by traditional dead reckoning and, if you were anywhere near a coast, by radio direction finding. I wasn't a professional navigator then, but was still perfectly comfortable with both methods, there wasn't going to be a problem on a trip of about 130 miles.

Heading north from the Channel Isles it isn't difficult to find the south coast of England, you just keep going and there it is; there's quite a lot of it. Our main electronic aid was something called a Kelvin Hughes Radio Direction Finder, a hand held device that picked up signals from a chain of dedicated Kelvin

Hughes transmitter stations around the coast. You tune in to each transmitter, confirm its Morse identification and then take a bearing on it; you then draw that line on the chart. One station alone isn't much help, you take three or four station bearings, and where the lines cross on the chart is your location. I was a ship's chandler and well familiar with this sort of equipment, I knew exactly how it worked.

Tom was doing the driving on this leg and I was doing the navigating. Heading North West from Guernsey I had confirmed our track was good with backward readings from the Channel Isles and Cherbourg transmitters, we were on course, the equipment was working fine and so was I. There was then a reception gap in mid channel before we started to pick up the south coast UK stations, and that was where it started to go wrong.

The Kelvin Hughes was powered up, but was now only receiving static or unidentifiable fragments. I persevered, switching it on and off and retuning different stations, but more out of annoyance that a brand new piece of equipment wasn't working properly, than from any desperate need for its information. It was midsummer and still daylight, I was confident I could find Fowey without any need for an electronic white stick.

Right on schedule the south coast of England showed itself across the horizon, the next step was to find a confirmed landmark, a headland, a river entrance, whatever. I had aimed to make our landfall just to the East of the Fowey River entrance, the cliffs along towards Polperro were easily identifiable, all we would need to do was to swing a little to the West and then home for tea.

We were not at this point desperate about the remaining daylight; but still it was by then around nine and there was only a finite time left before visual identification would become much more difficult in the dark; relying solely on lights and buoys. As we closed with the coast, the wind started to freshen, the forecast that morning in Guernsey had said that it would, but we had thought it would be too late in the day to bother us.

The coast line facing us looked unfamiliar, it was too straight and too regular. South Cornwall has a rugged coast line with a million inlets and granite cliffs rising steeply from the water.

This coastline wasn't like that, but we both knew that things can look different from the sea so we held our course for a while. At this point we were no more than mildly surprised by this failure to fix our location, we were confident of our abilities and knew we would sort it shortly.

The light was now beginning to fade and the wind continued to freshen. In the absence of a confirmed fix we decided to turn east and go with the wind, allowing ourselves to be pushed along the coast more rapidly: you never have far to travel in South Cornwall before you find a small harbour. By now we just wanted to get ourselves ashore, the people in whichever pub we ended up in would tell us where we were.

Unfortunately, despite scouring the land with binoculars, there were no harbours, large or small, just a continuous dull unbroken shoreline. The wind was now approaching storm force and there was hardly any light left. We considered pulling off to deeper water and riding the night out, headed into wind at low power, but we didn't have enough fuel for that. There was no option left but to close with the land, and take our chances on whatever we found.

We crept inshore with the very last glimmers of daylight marking where the sunset had been. Eventually we made out a slight wrinkle in the shore line, a small low headland marking what might have been the mouth of a small river. As we cautiously manoeuvred the boat into the partly sheltered cove, the last of the daylight faded completely.

Tom and I were by now in full waterproofs, with wind blown spray whipping in our faces and having to hold on as the boat bounced all over the shop. We dropped both our anchors, keeping the engine running until we were sure they were holding, and then let out an enormous sigh of relief. We hadn't discussed the possibility of just having to run the boat up whichever beach we came to, but I'm sure we both considered it.

Our dilemma then was that as we had informed the coastguard of our schedule, if we failed to report our arrival they would assume the worst and institute a search, if only for our wreckage. We felt there was no option but to go ashore and try to find a phone to let them know what was happening.

We had seen no houses on our way in and there were no lights visible, but even in a rural county like Cornwall there's only so far you can go before encountering human habitation.

We let the dinghy down from the stern davits and clambered in, we had decided it would need both of us to manhandle it through the line of surf that we could both see and hear crashing on the beach. I think there must have been a moon that night, there was certainly enough ambient light for some dim vision in the darkness.

We walked along the beach, heading inland and looking for any sort of path, as we did so we came across two young women and a young man in the surf.

The best way to describe their activity is to say that they were frolicking, or capering round in the shallow water, splashing each other and generally having fun, and all stark naked. Tom and I stopped and stared at them, and they stared back at us. The contrast between their lack of clothes and our full waterproof outfits must have looked odd to all parties.

Then with no more than a raised hand of greeting we carried on along the beach. It sounds unusual but even though it was the middle of the night, it was also midsummer, and if you can't go skinny dipping off a Cornish beach in midsummer, then when can you?

We found a path leading along the side of a field, sloping up from the beach. At the top of the field just inside a wooden five bar gate, there was an open two seater sports car, an MGB or similar. Obviously the skinny dippers' transport. At this point, if not sooner, we should have gone back and asked them to make the phone call for us, they had transport and we didn't; that would have been the easiest solution. Why this doesn't seem to have occurred to either of us I have no idea.

We climbed the gate and found ourselves in a narrow lane, at random we turned left and trudged along. In less than a mile, we came to a perhaps a dozen houses, forming a triangle around a patch of grass. All the houses were in darkness, but in the middle of the village green was a red British phone box with a light on inside it. Jackpot.

We dialled the Falmouth coastguard and explained our circumstances, they were grateful for the call and said that they had already flagged our boat as being potentially in trouble. It was agreed that we would ring them again as soon as we finally made it to Fowey. Duty done we made our way back to the boat, the skinny dippers had gone by then, so we never did get to invite them aboard for cocktails on the quarterdeck.

We passed the remaining hours of darkness drinking coffee and Courvoisier brandy from tin mugs and hoping that the anchors held. Around dawn the wind dropped away completely and was replaced by a thick mist, we sat and waited for the rising sun to clear it.

We waited for about two or three hours, but it showed no sign of moving, even though the sun was visible overhead. Eventually we'd had enough of messing around so we put up the radar reflector, got out the fog horn, weighed anchor, kept a close eye on the echo sounder and nosed our way slowly back out to sea.

After an hour of heading due South at walking speed, the mist finally lifted and so we picked up speed and headed West. It was rapidly and easily apparent that we were just off Looe and Polperro, in other words almost exactly where we should have been. Less than an hour later we were on a mooring in Fowey harbour.

Back at Tom's place I phoned the Falmouth coastguard again, to let them know of our safe arrival. They were relieved to hear me and said that they'd been on the point of organising a full search; lifeboats, helicopters, the lot.

'Well I did phone you last night, about midnight.'

'Not here you didn't.'

'Yes I did - it was me that spoke to you - I explained the whole thing, and said I'd call you again when we reached Fowey.'

No matter how much I insisted, he insisted even more strongly that they had never heard from me. He eventually said that the man who would have taken my call had just come back on duty, so he asked him. Still the same answer, Falmouth coastguard had not received my call. We ended the call politely, but with each of us convinced that the other was wrong, I knew I'd spoken to the coastguard and no amount of contrary assertions could change that. My comment as I replaced the receiver was, 'That man's a bloody fool.'

Then I had a brainwave, I could find out where we were last night by the simple expedient of locating the phone box. In those days all rural British telephone numbers had a telephone exchange, named after the local area, followed by a number; for example Saint Merryn 436. You then looked up in an area code book what the code for Saint Merryn was, which you then dialled followed by the number.

Although I have since forgotten, at that time I knew the name of the exchange from which I'd made the call, it had been written in the middle of the handset dial and was a typical Cornish name beginning with Saint. I read all the way through the area code book, but couldn't find the name. I then dialled the operator and asked her, but she said she'd never heard of it.

Resourceful to the end I scoured a large scale map of the Cornish south coast, again I drew a blank. I won't bother telling how successful my search of the local Admiralty Chart was in locating the shape of the cove we'd anchored in. And needless to say the Kelvin Hughes worked just fine the next morning.

I think this story sounds corny and predictable, I reckon that, as a reader, I could have guessed how it was going to end half way through, and I wish it didn't sound that way. I'm a fiction writer, and quite capable of making things up; but if I'd invented it, instead of reporting it, I would have introduced some sort of twist, to throw the reader off balance and add a touch of that nice word, verisimilitude. So what we're left with is a fairly standard ghost story which is only rendered remarkable by the fact that I know it happened to me and Tom.

What do I think was going on? My answer here puts me firmly amongst those backwoods Americans who claim to have been abducted whilst driving their pick up truck along a country road, and then sexually experimented on by aliens. It marks me out as a hopeless fruitcake, and once again I really wish that wasn't so, but not quite enough to make me pretend it didn't happen.

So I will whisper it very quietly and hope that no one I know is listening, but my best guess is that somehow Tom and I touched a parallel existence that night, an alternative reality. And if you think that sounds nuts - then I have to tell you - so do I.

But that isn't quite the end, there is one more interesting aspect to this, which is the reason why I felt it necessary to change my friend's name. Tom was with me throughout this experience, he saw everything that I saw, and he stood next to me in the phone box during my first call to the coastguard.

At each stage his bafflement grew with mine, right the way past me calling the coastguard a bloody fool and through to the end of the story, at which point it became quite obvious that there was no rational explanation that could cover these events. A sequence of events that had all taken place in the last 24 hours, and been witnessed by us both. At that precise moment he suddenly thought of a whole variety of reasons why what we had both just experienced could not in fact have happened, saying,

'You must have made some kind of mistake. - You must have misread the exchange name in the phone box. - The coastguard just forgot to log the first phone call and are now trying to cover themselves. - The

Kelvin Hughes just went on the blink for the afternoon, electronic equipment does that. - I'm sure that I could find our overnight anchorage on the chart, but I've got better things to do.'

This is a man I've known for most of my life, a man as rational as me, a man who has seen as much of the world as me, and someone whose judgement I would rely on; but if even such a man is determined to ignore the plain evidence of all his senses, he will.

The only time I ever mentioned it to him again, he was airily and laughingly dismissive. This dismissal was not prompted by any fanciful suggestion of mine about alternative realities, because I never made any such suggestion. That's the whole point, I never put it into words – precisely because I didn't need to. It was unavoidable and staring us both in the face.

Despite us having happily spent a great deal of time together on countless occasions since, the subject has never been raised again. Should he read this, I wouldn't want to offend him, but Tom's reaction manages the difficult feat of making my own opinion look like a model of rational good sense.

So far so good, and now we come to the last one; the shortest, the easiest and the most recent; but also the most improbable. Yet despite that, it is the most completely certain and significant, with not a single get out clause in sight.

I have never taken any instruction in meditation and don't plan to. I regard Western devotees of Hare Krishna and the more spiritual forms of yoga as naive and probably not very bright. I know that sounds arrogant, but I'm trying to be scrupulously honest, otherwise there's no point in any of this. However, despite such opinions I do practise a form of mind calming technique on myself. This involves me visualising my emotions as a deep rolling ocean swell, and my thoughts as the waves being blown across the surface, my aim is to calm the sea, to still the waters and with it my thoughts and emotions.

I use it most frequently in church, when I wish to use the occasion of the service to slow myself down and focus on what matters. I'm not sure it's religious in any way, it just happens that it's personally convenient and practical to use the service for that purpose as well as for the glory of God. Like so many of my actions, I suppose you could call it selfish.

The routine is that I use a passage of text, one of the exhortations to church attendance in the King James' version of the Communion service, or even a hymn where I don't know the tune and can read it as straight poetry. I then concentrate all my thoughts on every word and nuance of the passage, reading it internally as though I were addressing a packed Albert Hall.

I do this slowly and repetitively with as much concentration as I can manage, and as I do, I can feel myself relaxing, and the mental image of the sea surface calming down. My breathing, my jumbled thoughts and the visualised surface of the water all flatten out together.

Sometimes it works, sometimes it doesn't. Sometimes I find myself making notes about what I'm supposed to be doing at work on Monday morning, which, as you might gather, counts as a failure.

Ten years ago, in mid-summer, I was sitting in church just before the service began on a Sunday morning and had achieved a satisfying level of calm. I was focussed and receptive, with no surface clutter buzzing around the front of my mind, wide awake and fully aware of my surroundings. I remember that I was looking down the nave to the east window above the altar, at a scene of one of our previous Rectors preaching in foreign climes. And then, out of nowhere, my father spoke to me, my father who had been dead for two years, and to whom I never had the chance to say goodbye.

We needn't go into the tangled web of emotions, repressed feelings, memories of life's unfairness and so much of the usual psychological baggage that can surface at funerals. It was all there and I felt his loss deeply, but I wasn't fixated on the subject. There were aspects of our relationship that we had both regretted, but once he was dead I accepted that and tailored my memories and thoughts of him accordingly. On that Sunday morning, I hadn't thought of him recently and there was nothing in my mind or my immediate life to trigger any awareness of him.

As I sat in the pew, his words simply came into my mind. There was no audible speech, even internally in the way you can conjure up a friend's voice; so it would have been impossible for me to say that it sounded like him; there was no sound of any sort.

The words came directly into my mind, crisply, sharply and without any ambiguity, at the normal speed of human speech.

'I'm settled now, I understand why things happened the way they did, and I'm ready to move on.'

I took the last part to mean, as I'm sure I was meant to, not only that he was ready to move on, but that he was now going to do so. He didn't call me by name, he didn't say this is your father, he didn't say he loved me, he didn't say goodbye, he didn't say where he was moving from or to; all he said were the words I quote. To me the significance lay far less in the meaning, than in the fact that it had happened.

The words could certainly be applied to his life, and under the circumstances it was the sort of comment he could very well have wanted to make, but there was no peculiarity of the phraseology that was especially his, so how do I know that it was my father? I have no answer to that, I can't even take a guess, all I can do is to tell you that there has never been the slightest scrap of doubt, at the time or subsequently. I knew it was my father in the very split second the words began to emerge in my mind.

My reaction was one of profound shock, I was physically rocked back in the pew, if I hadn't already been sitting down I would have needed to do so. I made no attempt to reply or ask him a question, it would have been a waste of time, but then I don't know how I knew that either.

To nail down one possible loose end; nobody in my family would give a moment's credence to any form of spiritualism, it's deceitful nonsense designed for the gullible and the desperate, and I'm neither.

So I end up asking the same question in this case as the last one: what do I honestly think happened? There was no coastguard involved here, no malfunctioning radio direction finder, no alleged misreading of a chart; there are only three extremely straightforward possibilities; either I'm a complete liar, or I'm delusional, or my dead father spoke to me.

Just for once, I'm a step ahead of your here, as I already know the answer, but you can only read my words and decide for yourself which you think sounds the most likely.

None of the experiences described above have any immediate relevance to religious belief, there is nothing that I can see in them to make one believe in God. What they do, I think, is to remind you of an uncomfortable fact, a fact that many of you are probably already aware of. The fact that there is something beyond our every day human existence: something beyond that which we can reach out and touch. The problem lies in trying to work out what that is.

I don't know which is the more unusual, to have such experiences, or to acknowledge and recognise them? Tom can't be the only person who, when faced with a rational impossibility, decides the sensible course is to deny it ever happened. Effectively to close your eyes, put your fingers in your ears, say la la la very loudly and hope it goes away. Such a flight to a supposed and reassuring rationality can itself be escapist.

Our brains are hard wired to rationalise sensations, to make sense of the unusual, to fit unexpected things into familiar boxes, but that doesn't mean they're right. This phenomenon is why optical illusions work, you don't take a ruler to measure each of the lines in the drawing, you just say, it reminds me of that - so that's what it is.

It would seem that I have been lucky enough, sensitive enough or gullible enough, to have experienced some examples of the *unusual* in this world without making any special effort to do so. Such things have occasionally found me, rather than the other way round. If I have any gift at all, it might be to recognise them for what they are when I see them.

As Sherlock Holmes remarked: when you have eliminated the impossible, whatever remains, however improbable, must be the truth.

I don't know how widespread such things are, but other people must have experienced parallel, if not exactly similar episodes. The question is, did they accept them at face value, or just jab a finger at the mental Delete button?

Is there any short cut to seeing miracles – or seeing God? Mind altering drugs, once the preserve of witch doctors and more recently poets and artists, are now in widespread use almost throughout society. Does taking LSD connect you to God? I very much doubt it but can't honestly say, as I've never taken it, and the times I tried cannabis as a young man, it just sent me to sleep.

So how does a rather straight laced provincial like myself, who isn't on drugs and has no history of mental illness, come to have the experiences I've described?

Am I especially receptive or in some way insightful? It doesn't look that way to me, I have always thought of myself as being a bit of a plodder, I'm not intuitive, I'm not a visionary, there's not a flash of genius in sight. I'm the sort of man who always has to read the instruction book, who thinks predictability a virtue – I should have been an accountant.

CHAPTER THREE

How Dependable Am I?
- or how gullible?

At the risk of boring you, the only clues I can offer as pointers to my personality and character, and thus my reliability as a witness, come from some more episodes in my own life.

Unless you know me personally, your best measure of me might be a sight of how I act and react in stressful circumstances. It is at such times that our underlying personality is most visible. So how fanciful am I? How prone to wishful thinking? What events would have brought any such tendency to the surface?

The most obvious and dramatic of these would seem to be Margaret's diagnosis of cancer, then my own diagnosis twelve months later, and a couple of midair emergencies in aircraft. That should be enough to show up the more obvious fault lines in my personality.

All these things involved the prospect of death and seriously frightened me, but none of them provoked delusions or mystical experiences. I would like to be able to say that under the threat of approaching mortality I showed myself to be a cool and smooth operator, but that's not really how life works – is it? I'm afraid the best I can offer is a degree of stability and determination. My feet stayed firmly on the ground, or at least the cockpit floor, which I would suggest makes me far more likely to seek a rational explanation of strange events, before declaring anything a miracle.

Other people will see things differently, but in our experience of cancer once you get past the punch in the gut shock, it's not so much a fight or a battle, it's more a case of detailed hard work and application than anything else. The way we handled it there was very little high drama, it was almost a bureaucratic exercise. We were both worried and frightened, but after that, the overwhelming memory is of the loss of control and the hard work involved.

Getting the precise details of the diagnosis; going away to read about it, think about it and talk about it, and then going back with a written list of questions. Getting a second opinion where necessary and then agreeing a course of action, and finally doing it. All this at high speed and, if you've got one, with your wife or partner alongside you to stiffen the sinews and keep you focussed.

Margaret was first, and for a year it was her show with me in close support, and then it was my turn with the roles reversed. The point I'm making is that, despite the emotions and the pressure, we both stayed very grounded and realistic.

Yes, there were a couple of emotional wobbles, but there were no flights of fancy, no alternative Mexican cactus cures, no homeopathic nonsense. It was just a step by step hard slog, if ever we disagreed with a medical opinion it was always factually based, supported by solid mainstream evidence and then talked through with the people involved. Nothing wild and nothing wacky, and despite the constant pressure there were no visions.

I'm not saying that I won't ever give in to despair, if I feel the situation warrants it. The older you get, the more you accept that there might be circumstances where suicide is an option you could find yourself considering. I don't suggest or promote suicide as a cure for anything, but I do say that the irrationality of the act decreases with the years.

My point here is that had I possessed any inherent tendency to an easily reached state of despair or panic, it would surely have been manifest during those two years. My behaviour suggests a certain rather dull and clinical nature, quite unsuited to daydreaming or fantasy.

With the first aircraft emergency, it was entirely my own fault, which sounds familiar. Originally I had what's called a Private Pilot's Licence, which permits flight only when clear of cloud and in sight of the ground. The next step on my progress through the grades was to get something called an Instrument Meteorological Conditions Rating, which permitted flight in cloud. I had a trip planned from Manchester to Swansea in South Wales, there was high ground en route, but so what? Aircraft fly over high ground, it's what they're built for.

Halfway there I flew into cloud, the Met. office briefing had said it was there, but I was now permitted to fly through it, and so I did. Unfortunately, I hadn't read the Met. report carefully enough, particularly the part which had said there were embedded cumulo nimbus cells in the cloud cover. Those are thunderstorms which contain extremely violent and high speed up and down air currents. Whilst in cloud I flew into one of these cells, and then the aircraft really took off.

It hurtled upwards at a speed too great for the instruments to keep up with, viciously trying to shake itself apart, and rolling and turning as it did so. Every loose item in the cockpit flew across to stick on one side window, then smacked straight across to the other side, then to the roof, then to the floor, most of them hitting me as they passed.

All the instrument gyros had tumbled, and the display needles were shaking so much that no readings were possible. I knew what I'd done, that was obvious, but of no practical help.

I was as frightened as I've ever been in my life and completely certain that I was going to die, and yet in the middle of all this turmoil I still went through the check list for the situation; there's a check list for most scenarios in aviation and I knew the important ones by heart. The headline actions being to reduce power to avoid over speeding in the down draughts, switch off the auto pilot to avoid over stressing the control surfaces in the turbulence, and, as far as possible, to hold the control column loosely in a central position.

I considered writing a note of goodbye and apology to Margaret, but I couldn't have handled an eight inch whitewash brush in that maelstrom, let alone a pen.

When I finally fell out of the bottom of the cloud, I suddenly remembered there was a significant point I'd overlooked, namely, was the cloud base above ground level? Fortunately, although the hill tops on each side of me were in cloud, I had fallen into a valley, and had a couple of hundred feet of clear air in which to make my escape. Sheep sensibly scattered as I passed - to avoid early shearing.

I was drenched in sweat and carried on shaking, even after the aircraft levelled out. None of this demonstrates my cleverness, if I'd been even half way clever I wouldn't have put myself into such a stupid situation. Lucky certainly, in where I came out of the cloud, but also relatively unemotional, the plane was more volatile than me. All I exhibited was a degree of rather dogged determination.

The second aircraft incident was when we were departing Manchester airport bound for Bordeaux. We were climbing to our assigned level to join the Amber 25 Airway and head south, by this time I had a full Instrument Rating, and an airways equipped plane (i.e. professional level navigation and communication equipment) and thus could legally fly in any conditions. Passing through 5000 feet the engine blew up, and as that was our only engine a period of going downhill became inevitable.

Anyone with a hint of a personality would have given the first two verses of 'Nearer My God to Thee', followed by a couple of jokes on the way down and then greased a perfect landing in a field, whilst discussing what we were going to have to eat that night.

Instead of which, in my rather unimaginative way, I had to start going through check lists to make sure I was getting it all right. Switch off fuel pump, set best glide speed for range, make the Mayday call, get the local pressure setting and the ground wind, and all the other technical guff..

I'm sure it's all good stuff, but I cannot imagine anyone less likely than me to see visions, I really am the most improbable candidate for experiencing either the supernatural or the divine. If ever I see a shining light in the clouds it isn't the second coming of the Lord, it's just another plane heading our way.

With no power, our rate of descent was 750 feet per minute and we came out of the cloud base at about that height above ground level, which gave us the luxury of one whole entire minute to identify a suitable field, get lined up into wind, and then make our landing. Unfortunately, the countryside we found ourselves above offered a lot of power lines and trees but only a selection of small pokey fields, more suited to helicopters than fixed wing aircraft.

When making a forced landing without power, away from an airfield, if you're in an aircraft with retractable gear, you have an important choice to make. If you land with your undercarriage down you retain steering and braking ability on the ground, but run the very big risk that one of your wheels will hit or drop into something that will turn you over; introducing the unwelcome prospect of break up and fire.

Alternatively, if you choose to land with your gear up, to avoid that risk, you must recognise that the streamlined belly of the aircraft will allow you to slide uncontrollably for a considerable distance along the ground, which brings you back to the prospect of hitting something solid.

Luckily for me, I had, some time before, read an article in an American magazine called Flying (what else?), which had proposed a third method. Their suggestion had been that if you lowered your wheels and then, holding the wings level, deliberately stalled the aircraft at about fifty feet up, you should drop onto the ground hard enough to break off all three undercarriage legs in one go. This, it was reasoned, would give you the best of both worlds, with the broken stumps of the undercarriage bringing you to a rapid standstill in exactly the place you wanted to be.

Looking back, I can't believe that I was ever rash enough to try such a hare brained sounding scheme, but in the time available I couldn't think of anything better. Incredibly, it worked very well, our total ground run was thirty five yards. Allowing for the different weights of aircraft involved, that's about the same stopping distance you'd get from using the arrester wire on an aircraft carrier flight deck. So thank you to whoever wrote that article in Flying.

For what it's worth, the three of us onboard came safely through the landing in one piece and, once out of the plane, stood round in the field having a stiff drink from the bonded locker to celebrate.

At the time of the explosion, Margaret was sitting in the back of the aircraft, and after hearing the Mayday call on the intercom, as a pilot herself, understood as much as anyone about our situation and what needed to happen next. And so after I'd finished with Air Traffic Control, her only enquiry to me was,

'Are *you* alright?' And when I said yes, she went back to reading the paper, there isn't a lot to look at when you're in cloud, and the only visible action is on the instruments. Even so, I still haven't worked out if that was a display of confidence in me, or a professional master class in nonchalance.

As my co-pilot's day job was as a high priced fancy pants lawyer specialising in disaster litigation, (exactly the sort of person you *don't* want to give a nasty mid air fright to), we got an extremely good settlement for the wrongly fitted engine part which had caused the problem, enabling us to upgrade to a much larger twin engined aircraft.

If you'll excuse the diversion, there is another aspect of that incident which I found quite interesting, and which occurred a couple of hours later. It so

41

happened that when our distress call was received by Manchester Air Traffic Control, there was a four man team of Civil Aviation Authority crash investigators making a routine visit to the tower. They immediately decided that our emergency was too good an opportunity to miss and came straight out to the scene; along with the police, fire brigade and ambulance.

The endlessly hospitable farmer and his wife, in whose kitchen we had ended up, thought they'd been invaded. All these people wanted statements and information, and as the pilot, it all had to come from me. So for about two hours I was extremely busy being as professional and competent as I could manage, with everyone in sight. Eventually the level of activity receded, nobody was dead or injured, life goes on. It was then that I saw something I hadn't expected; both my hands were shaking uncontrollably and there were tears running down my face.

At first I just stared down vacantly at the scrubbed wooden top of the kitchen table, at my shaking hands and the dark splashes of my falling tears, I had no idea what was happening. Then the farmer's wife came over and helped me to my feet.

'Come with me, you're in shock.'

'What?'

'You don't have to talk to anyone any more, and now it's quietened down you're in shock, come with me.'

She took me through to the quiet of the front room, where she brought me another cup of tea and a cigarette, we did things differently in those days, and told me that I'd feel better shortly.

Ten or fifteen minutes later I was right as rain. I hadn't previously realised that being 'in shock' could be such an unavoidable and clear cut physical experience.

If I'd ever thought about it at all, I would have vaguely imagined that it was just an extension of pulling yourself together, or failing to. Perhaps this doesn't surprise you, but it did me.

As far as I can see, it is my very literal mindedness that makes me remember some of life's impossibilities rather than dismissing them. It is my rather boring doggedness which causes me to look as carefully as I can for reasonable and rational explanations to odd events, and then when I'm quite sure that there is no such explanation, to accept that the event was in fact unreasonable and irrational. It is that acceptance which is on display here.

Do I believe the government is concealing the fact that the earth is being visited by aliens? No I don't.

Do I believe there is mysterious vortex near Bermuda into which ships and aircraft disappear? No I don't.

Do I believe that a man can fly? Now you're just being silly.

Do I believe in miracles? If by miracle you mean some unusual or astounding event for which there is no currently available explanation, then yes, I do. Does that belief include such things as the possibility of Jesus walking on water? As I have already accepted the presence of the miraculous in my own life then yes, I don't see why not.

*****

One part of the cancer experience which has some relevance to my understanding of the sort of experiences I describe above, arose from the manner in which an epidural line had been fitted. I had cancer of the colon and the surgical routine is to cut out the diseased part of the intestine and then if there's enough of it left, they join the remaining ends back together; in medical terms it's called an anterior resection of the colon. This isn't keyhole surgery, it's from your pubic bone to your diaphragm - more like two hands and a bucket surgery.

In case you're interested, and aren't too squeamish, the bit I mentioned about joining the two cut ends of your colon back together, involves inserting a torpedo shaped device up your back end, where it, in some way, stitches around itself. It's curious what life turns up, I would never in a million years have imagined having a sewing machine shoved up there, let alone having it then switched on.

I asked the surgeon how they knew if the joint was secure, he said that while they had you open, they filled your abdominal cavity with water, then removed the sewing machine and inserted an airline up the same route, which they then turn on and look for bubbles. It's just like repairing a bicycle inner tube.

As well as the general anaesthetic you also have an epidural line fitted for the post operative delivery of morphine, it's all fairly straightforward. When I came round in the High Dependency Unit, all wired up and tubed up, the nurse explained to me that the setting on the epidural morphine would probably be sufficient as it was, but that if the pain was too bad I could press this button to temporarily increase the flow.

An hour or two later, when the final effects of the general had worn off, I was in significant discomfort and so pressed the button. It made no difference. This continued through the rest of the evening, and got much worse in the night.

I complained vociferously the next morning and the anaesthetist was wheeled in to deal with things. She gave me a finger wagging lecture to say that I was receiving enough pain relief to sedate a medium sized horse, and that I should stop being such a baby and just get on with things.

Suitably chastened I tried, and it's true that during the daylight hours, using every ounce of self control I could muster, the pain, whilst still significant, was just bearable. I later found that I had, at some stage, bitten my lips so hard they were bleeding. But during that second night it became much worse, I was shouting out and thrashing around the place, it was intolerable. The intensive care nurse took pity and, despite not being supposed to, gave me some tablets which took the edge of things.

With dawn, there was some reduction in the sheer intensity of the pain, and the physical exhaustion helped, but I knew that I couldn't cope with another night like that. I told the early morning duty doctor that if I was left in that condition again I would kill myself. He laughed,

'And how do you plan to manage that?'

'We're on the first floor, I'll go out of the window, and you won't stop me.'

He shrugged and left, but they then phoned Margaret to say that she needed to come in. It might have been their hope that she would help them out by telling me to shut up and get a grip, but that wasn't how it worked out.

When I next emerged from the delirium I found Margaret standing at the foot of my bed wagging *her* finger at the Consultant and a woman I later found to be the hospital manager. She was telling them that unless they got this sorted out, right now while she stood there and watched; she would sort *them* out. I found myself suddenly surrounded by people all gripped with an urge to be seen to do something; nurses, doctors, who knows, they could have had the car park attendant in there for all I cared. Then I heard someone say,

'What's this liquid on his bottom sheet?'

'I don't know, but it was like that the last time he was changed, I thought it was probably urine.'

'But he's got a catheter fitted.'

'Oh yes.'

It turned out that the epidural supply line hadn't been correctly attached to the tube going into my spine, and I'd been lying in a steadily deepening pool of morphine for the last thirty six hours. Not a single drop of the stuff had entered my body, I would have been better off licking the waterproof sheet I was lying on. At this point medical panic ensued - they could see the prospect of an extremely large legal action heading their way.

There were several exclamations of, 'Oh shit', none of which related to my faecal output. It was pure headless chicken time, a lot of people running around, wetting themselves and waving their hands in the air. One clear memory is the voice of my surgeon addressing the finger wagging anaesthetist from behind the folding screen near the door.

'You'll have to go in there and tell him.'

'I'm not going in there, you'll have to deal with it.'

'No, you have to go in there and tell him what happened.'

Then very loudly, almost shrieked. 'No, I can't talk to him – I won't.'

This was followed by the sound of her footsteps, actually running away down the corridor.

You can guess what happened next, this time they really did give me enough morphine to sedate a medium sized horse, they were trying to cover the fact that I'd previously had none, by now giving me too much; but as I'm sat here writing this, the overdose can't have been fatal. That's one of the things about a successful marriage; when the sh-- hits the fan you've got someone covering your back. In hospital things started to get more interesting.

I think I've always been able to direct my dreams, knowing that I'm in a dream and being able to steer it slightly this way or that. I have no idea if other people do this, trying to discuss your dreams with another person is a short cut to boring their pants off. I suppose it's just a question of the depth of your sleep or unconsciousness. The depth of sleep at which I usually dream seems to be such that I retain some vestigial self awareness, it has no other significance that I can think of.

What that meant was that when I slipped smoothly and gratefully into a painless drug induced hallucination I wasn't at all surprised to find that I was aware of what was happening.

'Oh great, a drug induced hallucination, I've never had one of these before.' I was completely stoned for the rest of the day, and grateful to have had the experience

For a completely different purpose, I describe a sanitised version of the lead up to this, and the sensations themselves in the first chapter of another book of mine; 'Loose Canon'. The only significant point I wish to make in this context is that thanks to a careless surgical error, I can now say with certainty that I know the difference between a hallucination and some of the other slightly non standard life experiences described in this book.

The hallucination itself was like a series of separate plays or stories, with me as the observer and central character, able to walk about and interact with those around me. Although it didn't feel odd at the time, all these experiences, unlike my dreams, were completely silent. Whenever I spoke with the other players I was simply aware that I was having a conversation and took it for granted that I didn't know what was being said, because it was part of the internal logic of the hallucination that I couldn't hear anything.

In the first sequence I was still in my hospital bed, in apparently the same room, with the same nurse at the same desk. I closed my eyes to sleep, but could still see the room. My brain told my eyes to open and then close again, but I could still see the room. It was then I realised that my eyelids worked fine, it was my brain that had gone walk about.

Looking at the room more closely I realised that the two windows that had been on the side wall were now on the end wall, but otherwise it was the same. Then I was driving a bus that turned into a ship; then I was in a friend's house, a place I knew well and visited often, and found that the room was actually no more than a stage set on some film studio lot, and that I could walk round the back of the scenery.

It was weird but sadly, not remotely exotic, and didn't even involve any sex. The experience was interesting as a novelty, but not sufficiently so to make me bothered about seeking a replay.

I cannot completely deny the power of the brain to convince us of a fantasy, one thinks of the long queue of people who have reported semi mystical end of life experiences; going through a tunnel towards a distant light, or floating above your own body in a hospital emergency room. I suspect that most, not all perhaps - but most, such experiences can reasonably be assumed to be products of the final random flickers of electricity through the neurons of a dying brain.

The fact that some of these 'dying brains' subsequently recover, with that dying memory intact, is surprising though welcome, but offers no proof of heaven or God.

With that in mind I obviously cannot swear beyond all possible doubt that I am immune to physical factors of which I am unaware. But to say that takes us to a level of probability where I equally couldn't swear that next Tuesday will be followed by next Wednesday; if pressed I would have to concede that the end of the world might intervene.

However, for all reasonable purposes, in light of my own perceptions and my own experiences, *which were usually in the company of other people*, I can state with confidence that I know when it's reality, I know when it's a dream and I know when it's an hallucination.

What we're left with is a man, me, who not only believes in the possibility of miracles, but further believes that he has very firm and rational grounds for doing so. A man who believes, even at the risk of sounding gullible, that he has had either the afterlife, or an alternative life, displayed to him.

You can begin to see why I think that as a religious believer I'm something of a fraud. What I have isn't so much faith, as a back catalogue of fairly cut and dried demonstrations, and that earns me absolutely no bonus points.

All I've ever done is to follow some very large and obvious signposts, any conclusions I've drawn have been more unavoidable than original. It is also worth noting that though my belief in events I am unable to distinguish from miracles does not on its own produce an automatic belief in God, it certainly removes a massive obstacle to such a belief.

CHAPTER FOUR

Monkeys on Steroids
- the curious vacuum at the heart of atheism.

There are times when I would find atheism to be a much more convenient and less taxing position than having a religious faith. On the surface, it appears to be rationally coherent and to fit all the observable data, but for me it leaves a lot of ground uncovered, and observable data isn't all the data there is.

The fact that I can't quantify unobserved data doesn't mean that it doesn't exist. I'm not sure where I'd go to find a bucketful of dark matter, but even if I did know, I would still think, so what? The truth is not all 'out there', a great deal of it is 'in here'. That means in your heart or in your head.

As a child I never wanted to be an engine driver, I always wanted to be a spaceman. I still secretly hanker after the Star Trek notion of, 'Exploring strange new worlds and seeking out new life and new civilisations. Boldly going where no man has gone before'. But alluring though the green haired women of Zarg might be, if I want to know more about life's central realities I'll look a little closer to home, I'll look at what's going on in my own head and in my own heart.

Atheism also fits the prevailing mood of the age. It is, apparently, a well known and scientifically proven fact that religious people are all either fanatical Muslims, fundamental Christians or pointless Buddhists. Or is it fanatical Christians, fundamental Muslims and aggressive Jews? I keep getting it mixed up.

One lot kills anyone they don't like, which seems to be most people, while another lot kills abortionists and have a priesthood that buggers small boys. If I didn't possess a religious belief to start with, then the level of smug unthinking complacency represented by that sort of comment would be quite enough to make me go out and get one.

But one can't damn such a widely held secularist view by being quite so elitist about the stuff that gets printed in mass circulation newspapers. Nor can you say that you look down on those who disagree with you, there are plenty of decent and actively good atheists. There are uncounted numbers of them who lead better and more moral lives than me, not a very high bar it's true. It's not that I'm better than anyone, it's simply that their answer to life doesn't suit or satisfy me, and it's not for want of trying.

There are several high profile regularly quoted atheists on the public scene at the moment, with Christopher Hitchens, A.C. Grayling, Alain de Botton and Professor Richard Dawkins as the more prominent examples. There are many areas of overlap between these writers but as Professor Dawkins seems to be the current leader of the celebrity atheist pack, it seems fair in this context to look at his work as being representative of the others.

He has written a lot about the folly of religion and the attractions of pure Darwinism. Well, I read a lot, and I'm of a curious disposition, so I've read his books – all of them I think, several more than once. I felt no urge to throw them violently aside, most are still on my study bookshelves, or in the hands of friends I've lent them to.

Professor Dawkins is a very clever man and an accomplished author, a persuasive advocate for his views. It is not my intention, or this book's purpose, to enter into a point by point rebuttal of those views, you can read him yourself and make your own minds up. However, in so far as Professor Dawkins' ideas have given me pause for thought, or simply caused me to say, 'Oh for goodness sake man!' Then they are worth mentioning.

There have been many articles detailing contradictions in his work, generally along the lines of: on page 65 of some book or other he says this, whilst on page 174 he quite clearly says that, followed by the cry of, 'Make your mind up Dawkins - which is it?' This is a foolish and pettifogging approach and doesn't interest me. I spend quite enough time detailing inconsistencies in the New Testament without wishing to adopt the same nit picking approach to the Professor, there are far larger items to disagree with.

In his best selling and most enjoyable book, The Selfish Gene, he posits the existence of what he calls a *meme*. This is an entity described as the cultural equivalent of a gene, and it's a device for replicating intellectual or social traits. Memes are described as spreading by imitation, so that when you hear a new tune, or a different way to build a mousetrap, your brain may be said to have been parasitized by that meme, and you can then go on to hum the tune or build the mousetrap.

He specifically and explicitly endorses the view that memes are living structures, not just metaphorically, but technically. These are not figures of speech, but physical entities, and it is at that point that he and I part company.

He develops his theme by suggesting that religious beliefs, along with patriotism and political beliefs, are spread by particular memes. The implicit suggestion being that none of us, except of course the Professor and his followers, are able to resist the onslaught of these virus like little critters invading our brains.

As a simile, the suggestion makes sense and if only he'd used a phrase like, 'It's *almost as if* there was something called a religious meme.' But he didn't, he made a point of playing it straight, as a scientific fact, and on that level it doesn't hold together.

It doesn't seem to have occurred to him that the spread of a religious belief in any culture could have been caused by people being persuaded of its worth, instead, we have the supposed fact that there must have been some pathological disturbance of their brains.

This description of the basis of religious belief may be characterised as the Laboratoire Garnier approach. If you use an impressive sounding name and chuck in some technical gobbledygook it should make your very basic product sound more sophisticated. And it can't be denied that the Professor's dislike of religion is very basic indeed.

It would be very easy to say that my problem with this is not that there's anything wrong with the theory, it's just that I'm too stupid to understand it. That would be an appealingly simple answer and one that I'm happy to consider, but I think it's worse than that. I think the problem is that I *do* understand it, and it's rubbish.

It's not so much that it, like the existence of God, is incapable of being demonstrated in a laboratory, as the fact that Professor Dawkins wishes to describe and discuss it as though it were more than a matter of faith, more than a Jesus style parable. He describes it as a matter of solid concrete fact, and that's a step too far.

I believe that Professor Dawkins has used his impressive qualifications and his immense public stature, to overawe any possible disbelief that this abstract thought is a tangible reality. He might as well be saying, 'If you're not as academically qualified as me in this particular subject, (and who is?) then you're not eligible to comment.' And if he doesn't say that personally, his acolytes certainly do, it's reminiscent of The Emperor's New Clothes.

Unlike the Professor, I am not an evolutionary biologist, I'm not any sort of biologist, but I do know something very large and very simple. That is that one doesn't need to be a time served cabinet maker to tell if a chair only has three legs and, as three legged chairs go, his religious meme theory is a gold medal winner.

If you seek to explain the persistence of religious belief then you might get some more useful clues by looking at a variety of high profile pronouncements through the years, all trying to make sense of man's position in the world.

Whether it's the Nicene Creed, which reaffirms that you can have your sins forgiven; the Magna Carta, which says that you cannot be unjustly imprisoned; or the American Declaration of Independence, is unimportant. All of them set boundaries and expectations that a man can live to. There is something deeply satisfying about knowing what you may hope to expect from life, and on whose authority. These are social and spiritual needs and not biological urges like food and drink; there is a difference.

The Declaration of Independence famously says, 'All men are created equal, that they are endowed by their Creator with certain unalienable rights. . .' To which your reaction could well be: Says who? All men are quite manifestly not created equal, some are tall, some are short, some are quick, some are slow; the list goes on. The only way in which all men are created equal is in the sight of God and, as a direct consequence of that, in the eyes of the law.

Some aspects of morality might be called rational benevolence, be nice to your neighbour and he might be nice to you, but such feelings are nowhere near as powerful as greed, envy and lust. No matter how many wrong turnings and deviations on the way, no matter how many deeply fallible men have screwed things up, the injunction to live a moral and lawful life has always been religious first and legal second. The one derives from the other.

Atheists can say till they're blue in the face that they would have thought of all this, if only they'd had more time, the fact is they didn't. Can it really be no more than a fluke, or is the wellspring of morality something outside the molecular construction of a human being?

Earlier mention of Professor Dawkins' acolytes brings up the Richard Dawkins Foundation, where so many of them gather, and where, for the payment of very large sums of money you can get the chance to have a meal, 'With Richard Himself'. As a personality cult it might not be quite North Korean, but it certainly has parallels with some of the Rolls Royce driving Indian gurus of recent years, where your closeness to The Master is decided by the size of your wallet.

On the subject of The Richard Dawkins Foundation, they do engage in some genuinely good works, helping the homeless and such like, which are presumably intended to make a public display of the fact that it isn't only religious people who can be charitable. It might only be a very small and poorly funded beginning, but they should still be congratulated for it. Whatever the motive, which I shall discuss later, the result of altruism is generally a good thing.

From which you can take it that I am unimpressed by the Professor's suggestion, in The Selfish Gene, that altruism is simply the behaviour that best enables genes to survive.

Replacing a human instinct for good with a biological imperative is only a step or two away from introducing those other biological imperatives; eugenics, euthanasia, abortion and the forcible sterilisation of undesirable elements. Welcome to the party.

Where things start to look less benign is when you take a look at the on line discussion pages associated with The Foundation, and other similar on line sites. The two prime subjects are obviously the validity of the central Dawkins/Darwinian view and man made global warming. On both subjects there is an establishment view from which no dissent is tolerated.

The standard response to any criticism is invariably some version of, 'You're just too stupid to understand', accompanied by a good deal of sneering sarcasm. There is remarkably little discussion, rational or otherwise, but an awful lot of bludgeoning. In fact the sheer virulence of the abuse directed at dissenters can only be understood by the realisation that you are dealing with a religion, and that any attacks on their views are seen as heresy.

Their veneration of The Master is vaguely unhealthy and somewhat medieval. Perhaps, when the Professor finally dies and goes to nothingness, which one hopes is long in the future, fragments of his bones will be kept in jewelled reliquaries as holy relics, and brought out once a year to be marvelled at.

I'm afraid the Professor is just too evangelical for my taste, too prone to anger when crossed. He is the atheist version of the Leviticus quoting Christian fundamentalist ranter, a man who's seen the light and knows he's right and can't wait to tell you about it; again and again and again.

I've tried to develop an enthusiasm for his point of view and I don't disagree with the idea that Darwinism, although incomplete, is more complete than other current evolutionary theories; just as long as you don't ask the missionary zealots what happened *before* the big bang.

I've laid myself open to his arguments, and some of them are quite persuasive, I've read the books, I've read the articles and even some of the endless on line discussion pages, but it just hasn't taken - it simply wasn't enough. Their creed is not all there is, and it isn't just that it denies the existence of God, it's more that it denies the existence of a soul, and on that point alone I'm convinced they're wrong.

Blind faith, which I hope is not the sort I have, might be bad, but it's nowhere near as bad as the blind rejection of faith, which is mad.

When confronted with the blank stone wall certainty of supercilious correctness, which is the atheists' most common identifying feature, I find some phrase such as, 'Wake up and open your eyes.' floating to the surface. An urge to tell them that they don't have to swallow the prevailing dogma, original thought is still possible, and sometimes even helpful.

It's the same when you're assured by a man made global warming fanatic that, 'The Science Is In.' Then you know you're in the presence of a very small and firmly closed mind. According to preference you may either pat them on the head or kick them up the backside, but don't, whatever you do, take any further notice.

I remain unconvinced that when confronted with the proverbial bucket of green primeval ooze, steaming gently in the sunshine, with the occasional bubble going plop, and told that if it gets struck by lightning a few times and I stick around for long enough, Shakespeare will eventually step out and brush himself down. Yes, I know that's a bit reductionist but it isn't unfair.

When push comes to shove, I find myself incapable of taking that last great leap of faith into atheism, and although that inability, in itself, would not necessarily oblige a belief in God, that is where I find myself.

I mean no insult to the man when I say that none of the hundreds of thousands of carefully crafted words in Professor Dawkins' many published works, and he's no slouch, come anywhere near the restrained beauty, clarity and emotional impact of the King James' version of the 23rd. Psalm, or the Nunc Dimittis. The two of which added together come to less than two hundred words. Please don't say that such literary heights were not his objective, were he capable, it would have shown.

What might be less obvious is why that is? Is it for no better reason than that the Psalmist and his translator were better poets or better stylists, or is it that their work was divinely inspired? It's an unanswerable question, but it arises every time one looks at a work of genius.

Some people might not wish to acknowledge the presence or influence of the divine in this world, or anywhere else, but other than the wilfully blind, there must be very few people who've never seen signs of it. Were I ever to produce work of that quality I would cut the plug off my computer, break every pen in the house and never write another word; not even a shopping list, not even goodbye. Sadly, I reckon my pens are fairly safe.

As I've said, some of the unusual events described here, even though defying rational explanation, could simply be taken as proving the world to be queerer than we know, and do not themselves prove the existence of God, and yet I still believe there is a God. Why is that? What is it that takes me from an acceptance of the miraculous in this world to a belief in a supreme being, a creator, an enabler? Then going further, from that belief to the acceptance of the Christian God?

The first step is fairly straightforward and involves little more than looking at the world, with its combination of deep complexity and simple beauty, and then asking myself if this is no more than the result of entropy? Entropy, at its most basic level, being that tendency in nature to move from order to disorder. If you build a tower of dominoes and then knock it over, it won't fall into a neat rectangular stack of dominoes, it will fall into a jumbled heap; that's entropy.

I am aware that the theory of natural selection is said to override such a tendency to chaos, with random and accidental changes in an organism providing it with a reproductive advantage, where such variants prove beneficial. I also accept that such adaptive evolution can require the passage of geological aeons to produce major changes in the species mix.

Well let's just say that I'm prepared to wait that long, I'll take the collected works of James Joyce, a large bottle of San Pellegrino and a folding chair, and then I'll sit there - and I'll wait. Some waits turn out to be fruitful and some don't, and I think this one will be in the second category.

Will the achingly slow accumulation of beneficial mutations really be faster than the natural tendency of this world to fall apart? Is that really the whole and complete story? It could be the limited breadth of my stunted imagination that's letting the side down here, but I can't climb onboard with that proposal. I can't cope with the routine attempt to gloss over the move from reactive impulse driven animals to sentient humanity, as if the distinction between the two was no more than the evolutionary step of amphibians moving onto land.

The separation between animals and men is more than a matter of degree, they are different categories of creature. There is a huge difference between an aardvark and an ant, but that is as nothing when compared to the difference between a monkey and a man. It is a frequently repeated assertion that we are all animals, naked apes, and that the only significant distinctions between mankind and monkeys are the toys we play with and the houses we live in. I don't believe it; a man writes poetry, a monkey never has and never will, they are not simply variations of the same thing.

We might very well all have developed from the primeval ooze, but we developed into very different beings, and to aggressively, and repeatedly insist that there was nothing miraculous about any of this is a head in the sand position. Saying, in a deeply meaningful voice, as though it were some profound insight, that dolphins are more intelligent than human beings is a disservice to both species; no more than a fashionable affectation, and a damn silly one at that.

According to the internet I share 95% of my DNA with a chimpanzee, 90% with a cat and 50% with a banana, yet I promise you that I'm none of those things. Such a relationship might sound close, but other than being briefly curious, it is utterly irrelevant. Although if I absolutely must be a banana, I would rather be a Caribbean banana than a South American banana - it should save me learning Spanish.

If all you can say of the intellectual and spiritual complexity of human beings, and their sheer range of achievements is, 'Oh they're just monkeys on steroids,' then it really isn't my imagination that's failing to cope. As Q was prone to remark in the Bond films, 'Do pay attention 007.'

It should be observed that it needs only one of the apparently inexplicable events described earlier from my own life, or a similar event in anyone else's life, to be 'true', in other words to be exactly what it seemed to those who were there at the time, to put a fox in the evolutionary hen coop.

Once you have established that there are events in the development and emergence of humanity which are quite manifestly not accounted for by Darwinian evolution, then this doesn't so much disprove the theory, as to point out that the theory is massively incomplete.

And I don't mean incomplete in a manner already acknowledged by Darwinians, in that there is some detailed work around the edges still to be tidied up; I mean an incompleteness which is central and perception changing. I can't tell what that thing is, but I can tell you with certainty that it is something significant. What is perhaps less certain, but still looks likely to me, is that the 'significant missing something' just happens to include the human soul, or if you prefer, the human ability to write poetry. The difference between the noblest animal on the planet and the basest human being is not a mere detail.

Having established my belief that human beings have souls, you can call such a thing a spirit if you want, I should offer some definition of what I mean by that. This is an almost impossible thing to do, trying describe something intangible that you only know of by inference. I mentioned the ability to write poetry and that's certainly part of it, along with the ability to grasp, discuss and act on abstract concepts. Then consider also attributes such as faith, hope, love, ambition, loyalty, fairness and dignity, these are not animal characteristics but part of the essential essence of humanity.

If, as I believe, there is such a thing as life after or beyond death, then the soul is that part of you that lives that life. It is the part of all of us that means we really are more than just monkeys on steroids.

What it boils down to is that there is something there beyond the nuts and bolts, something that you won't find in a post mortem examination. If there is anyone wishing to stamp their foot at that, and say they won't believe in anything that they can't prod with their finger, or pick up and wave about, then God help them. Such people must inhabit a sterile and purposeless wasteland. The attributes of faith, hope and love are not the workings of a selfish gene.

I don't know if I need to say it, but I can promise you that I didn't start any of this with an existing prejudice and then chop the facts to suit, but rather came to the positions I lay out in this book slowly and reluctantly, driven by a lifetime's worth of unavoidable clues and pointers. Frankly, I'd far rather be messing around on a Devon beach with Jack and Charlie, my grandsons, or even mending that broken gutter on the garden shed.

So do I believe in God? Yes I do, I can think of no better explanation for the world I see around me. As I've just explained, for me it's the only reasonable answer to a lot of questions. This doesn't mean that I have all the answers, nowhere near, but I do know that I reject the atheist answer as untenable, and am long past hiding myself in evasive agnosticism. The existence of sentient humanity without a supreme being seems to me to be far too high a level of improbability.

CHAPTER FIVE

An Unfortunate Beginning

I was born in Salford in the North of England, the second son of hard working and prosperous parents. My paternal forbears, for the previous three generations had all been engaged in our family ship's chandlery business; the men were all boozers, womanisers and gamblers but as I say, also hard workers, and with a useful talent for turning a profit.

It was considered normal for the male head of the family to have his wife and children in one house, and then a kept woman in another house. My father had Betty, his father had Ada and his father had Nellie Bethel. Although this situation was openly acknowledged by all parties, it was not a happy state of affairs, with all the suppressed resentment and emotion you might expect, simmering just below the surface. Then when it stopped simmering it would boil over, and there would be another wall shaking row, with conveniently small items of furniture being hurled by all parties. I was in my teens before I discovered that nests of tables were not in fact designed primarily for throwing.

On the maternal side the situation was less prosperous and as a consequence more straight laced; the men and boys worked down the pit and the women and girls worked in the mill. Which pit and which mill didn't matter, your destination was determined by history and your gender, the steam roller of the social order then pressed you firmly into place. As the hymn puts it, 'God made them high and lowly, he ordered their estate.' The fact that my mother married my father was considered by her family to be more remarkable than an orthodox Jew marrying a Gentile.

We left Salford to live in Cheshire when I was about five years old, my father needing to be closer to Liverpool, where he had opened a new branch of the family business. Then at the age of seven we moved into what would be our 'family home', a large Victorian pile on the Wirral, with a three acre garden, a long sweeping drive and a butler's pantry. When my father's father, Horace, arrived for his first visit, his only comment, beyond a derisive snort, was, 'The higher a monkey climbs the tree the more he shows his arse.'

Which, even at that age, I thought was frankly a bit rich, considering that he had just stepped out of a chauffer driven Buick limousine (they were always Buicks, I don't know why), with his bottle blonde diamond dripping fancy woman in tow.

However, family opinion accepted that fancy women were a fact of life, meriting no more than a resigned shrug, and as Horace had lost his licence so many times, the chauffer was a necessity rather than a luxury. Besides which, my brother and I used to love nothing more than sitting in the kitchen with Albert, the chauffer, listening to his wartime tall stories. And so whilst the grownups got drunk at one end of the house, we would sit round the kitchen table re-enacting

Rommel's downfall in the Western Desert, and hearing of Albert's crucial role in the proceedings.

*****

But all of this is a diversion, what I need to look at next is the background to my beliefs, both moral and religious, which is rather more difficult than arguing with Dawkins or explaining why I believe in miracles.

What is the connection between experience and religious belief? What makes me think that there is not just a God, but a specifically Christian God? There are far too many excellent *bad* reasons to be a Christian, lots of which apply to me, so I shall attempt to strip those away and see if there's anything left at the end of that. And that means taking a slightly longer look at my upbringing, at that point I suppose we shall have covered both nature and nurture.

The first and most obvious reason for me being what I am now is because I was born in England, and brought up as an Anglican, in an occasionally church going family, and at ostensibly Christian schools. My parents took it for granted that church attendance was a good thing and so, when younger, I went to Sunday School, and when a little older accompanied them to church, whenever they could be bothered to go.

I didn't resent or dislike this, it was just the way the world worked. I listened to the stories and whilst I wasn't seriously engaged by them, neither did I consciously reject any of the teaching. In Geography I was told that Canberra was the capital of Australia and in church that Jesus died for our sins, I didn't much care about either issue, so why would I pick a fight on the subject?

Most of my education, from the age of about nine, was at a boarding school, King William's College in the Isle of Man, and although seriously brutal and abusive by modern standards, it was not, perhaps, especially so for its time. In those days school discipline was always applied with the cane or the fist. If artillery is the last argument of kings, then in those days brute force was often both the first and the last argument of school masters. Hitting children was the standard response to a wide variety of circumstances throughout the British educational system.

Three times a year my mother would deposit me, and my large cabin trunk, either at the Liverpool Pier Head, from where the Isle of Man Steam Packet Company would take me on a four hour ferry trip; or at Liverpool Airport from where British European Airways or Manx Airlines would take me by air, to the Isle of Man. Then ten or twelve weeks later the process would be reversed.

For those with an interest in such things, the aircraft I occasionally flew to school in provide a guided tour through mid twentieth century aviation. The De Havilland Rapide, a 1930's canvas covered seven seater bi-plane; the Dakota, that workhorse of the Second World War; the Bristol Freighter, which looked like a flying whale, rattled insanely and had a howling gale blowing through its forward opening cargo doors, and finally the luxury of the turbo prop Vickers Viscount. Obviously the school sports teams' Away Fixtures, on The Mainland, required similar arrangements. It was all rather like getting to and from Hogwarts.

Whatever the transport, school was the reality of my life, where I spent most of my time and had all my friends; holidays at home were no more than fleeting intervals between the terms.

You might think that finding your parents wanted you to go to a boarding school in what was, effectively, another country could depress a child. My belief then, and now, is that my parents genuinely thought the arrangement offered the best available education, and that I would benefit from it. That was the general perception of boarding schools at the time, and it's true that I did benefit, though not perhaps in the ways they had imagined.

The College's approach to Christianity, to life and to anything else, could be summarised by the single word: robust. In the summer term the day began with a compulsory seven o'clock length in the school swimming pool, always naked, to avoid any messing around with wet costumes. There was a church service in the school chapel every morning, and two on Sundays.

If nothing else they were amongst the few guaranteed times in the week when you weren't being run ragged to *do* something, usually something horribly energetic. The school chaplain was a deeply unspiritual man, whose approach to empathetic counselling was exemplified by his threat to rip one boy's arm off and beat him to death with the soggy end.

One evening after lights out, two friends and I had cycled illicitly to Douglas, the island's capital, to see an X rated sex film. Pornography had to be really worked at in those days, with a ten mile bike ride each way in the dark, leaving very little energy for self abuse. When the lights went up at the end we discovered that the school chaplain had been sitting three or four rows in front of us, for a moment we stared directly at each other and we thought we were in deep trouble, though perhaps unsurprisingly, we heard no more about it.

Had we been more worldly wise, we would have probably blackmailed him, the little thugs that we were. I've never blackmailed a vicar, yet - it's still on my To Do list. As I say, it was all rather robust.

My education was, in its own dissolute way, highly successful, wide ranging and varied but almost completely non curricular. Smoking, drinking, spending long hours in pubs, early fumbling with girls, shoplifting, betting on the horses which was then illegal and driving whilst unlicensed, underage, uninsured and drunk. In other words, treating any rule of the school, or law of the land with contempt, wherever we thought we could get away with it.

On one occasion, I was obliged to flee the scene of a road traffic accident, by legging it across country in the middle of the night, as the car I had driven through the drystone wall of a field was a rental car that we had 'borrowed', complete with its keys, from a hotel car park. I say none of this proudly or defiantly, once again it was just the way things were. I wouldn't describe myself as completely feral, as I could tidy my act up when necessary, but I was certainly running wild in an environment that, unwittingly, allowed for such a thing.

My own behaviour was not exceptional, I did none of these things alone, all my friends behaved in like fashion. I imagine things are managed differently these days, it's all probably very nurturing and caring, but when I was part of it, the English public school system bore an uncanny resemblance to William Golding's book, The Lord of the Flies. It might not have been a desert island we were 'stranded' on, but the effect was similar. If ever I get thrown into a cockroach infested hell hole of a Venezuelan jail, I shall feel comfortably at home.

One of our less offensive activities sometimes took place on Sunday afternoons. If there was nothing else happening we would cycle over to a ruined mill and witchcraft museum, two or three miles away at the back of Castletown. This was the Witch's Mill, run by an elderly gentleman called Gerald Gardner, who was, in a small way, moderately famous and often referred to in newspaper articles as The Founder of British Witchcraft. The place was a strange mix of shrunken heads and carvings of such things as The Great Horned Beast of Beelzebub, but with an attached coffee bar and the only juke box in the area. (I can't resist the cliché - the Devil has all the best tunes.)

You might agree with me that spending time in this place, enlivened by occasional appearances of the wild haired and self styled 'Doctor' Gardner, knocked spots off whatever it was the school imagined us to be doing at the time.

But the clincher was that the coffee bar was where some of the local girls also hung out on Sunday afternoons. In retrospect it was probably as well this was a long way from home, as the girls in question were every bit as rough as we were, and considerably more mature. Despite the surface bravado, it gives a fair indication of my underlying immaturity to remember my embarrassment at first hearing reference to the periodic use of something they called manhole covers, and realising what was meant.

In contrast to the louche and bogus hocus pocus of the Witch's Mill on Sunday afternoons, Sunday night Evensong in the College chapel could sometimes be very high church. One of our regular visiting preachers was a high ranking Manx clerical dignitary called the

Reverend Fred Cubbon, known to one and all as Pious Fred.

I have no wish to denigrate the man's memory, as he could well have possessed many excellent qualities, beyond those evident to me. Nonetheless he was, in appearance, a florid and fleshy man with full and glistening lips, which he regularly moistened with the tip of his tongue, an unctuous manner and more jewellery than the Queen Mother. His pectoral cross alone was a gem studded marvel of expensive bad taste and would clank heavily against the pulpit lectern as he leaned forward to address us, 'Now boys . . .'

Fortunately, I'd been in the Boy Scouts and so knew all about camping. I thoroughly enjoyed his visits, they were even better than Blood and Thunder Jenkins, the bible thumping vicar of Malew; though how such a man as Pious Fred was ever thought suitable to preach at a boy's school must forever remain one of life's small mysteries.

Another memorable figure was the school doctor. Doctor Scott Forrest, (perhaps that name should take a hyphen – who knows?) a Highland Scot who both looked and sounded like Private Fraser from Dad's Army. He always had a lit cigarette in his mouth, which swung all over the place as he talked to you around it. The fascination lay in the half inch or more of ash on the end, and as he conducted the examination, usually of a rugby injury, you would find yourself watching the ash and waiting for it to drop off. By the time the ash was more than an inch long you'd be incapable of looking at anything else, but then at the very last moment he'd casually take it out, shake the ash on the floor and then jam it back in. It was better than hypnosis.

It was he who let me in on a great medical secret, which I now pass on with my compliments. 'You keep your feet and your dickie clean and dry, mind you I said clean and *dry*, and all three of them will work pairfectly.' Imagine that in a Highland accent, with both his eyebrows and the cigarette end all operating independently. Whatever the ailment, the answer was always a white granular ointment called Balmosa which was rubbed vigorously into the affected area. I don't remember any of us ever catching malaria, but had we done so I'm sure that Balmosa would have dealt with it. They don't make doctors like that any more, which I genuinely think is a great pity.

The study system, where between three and six boys from the same house were allocated a study to share was an excellent idea. This place became your living room and work space, where you kept all your personal possessions, with a shared toaster and electric kettle. It became almost your home from home, and even if your study mates weren't your closest friends, all your foibles and peculiarities were known and tolerated, as if in a family.

Scientific experiments were conducted here; the interested party would take a pair of dividers and insert one of each of the pointed ends into the holes of an electrical socket, and attach a pair of braces to the on/off switch. Then at the full length of the braces, pull the switch on, and observe the resulting explosion cause the dividers to bury themselves quite deeply into the opposite wall.

Next to our study there was a large sort of internal courtyard, called the Octagon, and if the wind was in the right direction we would wedge open the door leading from the open air into the Octagon. We then opened our study sash window about twelve inches at the top, and even with our door shut this produced a strong draught blowing through the study, a state of affairs known as Blow Through. In this condition smoking was perfectly possible and quite undetectable.

Betting on horse races was illegal in those days, unless you were at the actual race course, and illegal off course bookies were routinely raided by the police. This situation was clearly understood and equally clearly ignored, by all. Every morning Alf, the lavatory cleaner, would clatter along the red tiled floor of the study corridor, using his mop to push a large galvanised bucket, and stopping in each of the studies would pick up that days bets and drop off the previous day's winnings. How the school authorities can have remained unaware of these activities is beyond me, it's not even as if any of the parties involved were being very careful.

The school was an exclusively male establishment, all the house masters were unmarried and in some way psychologically damaged goods, refugees if you like from the real world going on out there. I assume there was some sodomy, but it was not overtly widespread and seems to have passed me by.

Would I have lent a hand, if they were ever a man down, as it were? I don't think so, but in that hormone rich environment it's difficult to be certain, anyway I'll never really know as I wasn't asked. I suspect that I just wasn't pretty enough, but then, that has so often been my downfall. An awareness that such an ambiguity even exists is enough to make it difficult to be condemnatory on the subject.

The only scholastic saving grace during my school days was that I read a lot, anything and everything. One of my early form teachers, when I was nine or ten, was the admirable Mr. Cash, and I owe him a great deal. He would spend part of each lesson reading us episodes from novels, The Black Tulip by Alexander Dumas was one I remember, and also some of Sir Walter Scott's Waverley novels. He would not only read a portion of the text, but would also give us some of the historical background. I was fascinated and, interestingly, didn't realise that the books in question weren't children's books, but full length adult novels.

By the time I was twelve I had read for myself, amongst many other books, all four volumes of Mikhail Sholokhov's weighty Russian classic 'And Quiet Flows the Don', and that was for pleasure not for work. This might not be exceptional in academic surroundings, but in the coarse, rugby playing, cross country running, anti intellectual world I inhabited, it was I think slightly unusual.

In the classroom there was a group of subjects, the arts subjects such as English, History, Geography, Scripture, Art, where I would always come somewhere near the top of the class no matter how little work I did. Then there were the sciences and foreign languages where I would always come somewhere near the bottom, no matter how *much* work I did. In maths I was ignored and the class went on without me, in French I was told to sit quietly at the back and left to look at a pile of old Paris Match magazines, while the rest of them mangled their irregular verbs. I suppose I should have been put out by this dismissive treatment, but to be honest I was quite happy with the arrangement. 'You don't bother us Okell, and we won't bother you.'

Some years later I discovered that I had learnt far more of the French language and about French life from the magazines, than the rest of them had from the irregular verbs. A similar surprise awaited me with maths, when I began to study navigation.

The only clues that I had any scholastic abilities that weren't covered by the curriculum came unwittingly, from people trying to demonstrate the exact opposite. In an English lesson, the master had circled the word 'beam' in one of my essays, so I asked in class why he'd done this. He replied that the word in question had many meanings; a structural timber, a ray of sunshine, a smile, a searchlight beam, but none of these applied in the context that I had used it. I pointed out that it also meant the width of a boat, which had been what the passage referred to. So he picked up a dictionary and looked the word up, read the entry to himself and then summoned me to the front of the class, where he had me read it out in full. There was no reference to the width of boats and class hilarity ensued at my stupidity.

The thing about this incident which still astonishes me, is not that he possessed the only dictionary in the world not to have included the meaning I had employed, or even that he was ignorant of it himself, but that I was so completely unsurprised to find that I knew something that he and his dictionary didn't. I simply took it for granted that was how things were. Self confidence at that level, in a child, is worryingly close to arrogance, and as I wasn't smart enough to have covered it up, I must have got quite a long way up some people's noses.

Another incident which made a similar point was in history, a subject I was good at, but one where the master, a man called Boyns, and I hated each other openly and unreservedly. I never quite worked out why he hated me, unless, of course, it was connected to my comments at the end of the previous paragraph, about what an arrogant little sod I was.

In my turn I loathed him because he was a swaggering lout and a bully, a man with favourites, who only responded well when people sucked up to him. If ever I were to meet someone with a good word to say about this man, I would have immediate and serious doubts about their character.

Despite his apparently interesting war service, he had become the embodiment of that phrase: a man amongst children but a child amongst men. His routine was to pick on one of the weaker boys who found the subject difficult, and then taunt them about their supposed lack of intelligence, working the room to raise a sycophantic laugh at the victim's expense.

Whenever he was too tired and emotional to teach us any history, or too bored to tell us another of his stories about the hairy deck landings he and his Corsair (a big single engined fighter - look it up if you're interested) had made on carriers in the war, he would tell us to go away and write an essay. Any essay we liked, it didn't matter if it was historical, it was just something to shut us up and keep us occupied. After one such exercise, we were all sat in class and he had our books piled up on his desk. He sorted through them with studied casualness until he came to one, which with a mock cry of delight he pulled out, it was mine.

I was told to stand, as Boyns launched into a tirade of abuse about how much he hated cheating, how people who cheated were the lowest slimiest form of human life imaginable, how cheating poisoned the well of all honest human endeavour. It went on for some time, and all the time he was saying this he was pacing about, brandishing my exercise book like a weapon, and yet still looking directly at me, but I hadn't a clue why.

I had no moral objections to cheating and had cheating ever suited my purposes I would probably have done so; the rather depressing fact is that I just didn't care enough about school work to bother. And anyway, this was an essay - how can you possibly cheat with an essay? You just make the damned thing up don't you? I soon found out.

'Okell here thinks that he can copy someone else's work and simply pass it off as his own. He thinks that I'm so stupid that I can't tell the difference. Well I'll tell you Okell, I might not know which book or magazine you copied this from, but I can certainly spot a cheat - and that's what you are.'

With that he walked over to the waste paper basket beside his desk and ritually ripped my exercise book into fragments before dropping them into the bin. I was delighted, it was the first time that anyone had ever suggested that my work was of a professional standard. He provided my first good review, and never mind the circumstances - you take them where you find them.

A note about the masters at school having favourites, looking back it's surprising just how far that system extended. In every class there was a group of three or four boys who would, between them, be awarded every single prize; every year it was the same group. Sometimes the exact arrangement of the distribution would change. Blenkinsop Minor would win the Enid J. Bagnold prize for Scriptural Knowledge and the Arthur Futwell prize for Mathematical Excellence this year, whereas next year he would collect for Geography and Overall Effort. But it was always the same small group that scooped the pool.

The result was that Prize Giving Day, or Founder's Day, or whatever they called it, was of no interest to the great majority of the pupils, most of whom just talked amongst themselves, completely ignoring the events on stage. This situation fostered a widespread degree of contempt for the whole system, and while you may say that I already possessed that contempt, in spades, they need not have played quite so openly to my weaknesses.

Speaking as someone who has been an employer for most of my adult life, I think this is a desperately unproductive way to treat either staff or schoolchildren. It's not just that it annoys people, you don't get anything back from them and you don't involve them - and if you're any good at your own job, you should be doing both.

There was another episode with the man Boyns, which I had almost forgotten until now, and one which shows him in a very slightly less jaundiced light. I took the exams which in those days we called 'O' Levels, one of which was in History. For someone with a natural interest in the subject, and who read a lot, in other words me, the questions were extremely easy. The only issue when I'd finished the paper was something along the lines of; did I score ninety five percent or ninety eight per cent? Yet surprisingly, when my results arrived during the summer holidays they said that I'd failed.

This presented a minor problem as I was supposed to be taking English, History and Art in the sixth form, and the idea was that you should have passed these subjects at 'O' Level. So the next term, on our first encounter in the sixth form I raised the matter with him. This prompted another of his outbursts.

'Oh for God's sake Okell, just what is it that you're trying to prove here? Do you expect them to give you a medal or something? You and I are both perfectly well aware that you can do the blasted subject, who cares if the examiner was drunk?'

The matter was never raised again, and I didn't appeal the result, I don't think you could in those days - you just had to take whatever they dished out. To be honest I rather agreed with his assessment.

Anyway, none of that mattered much as I left school after one or two terms in the sixth form. I had discovered that, despite what the careers master had told me, it wasn't necessary to have an Art A Level to get into art school, you simply turned up on their doorstep with a portfolio of your work, and if they liked it you were in, and if not, you weren't. So that was what I did.

Years later, one of my friends learnt where I had been 'educated' and expressed astonishment. He said that his own school, who at one time used to play us at rugby, had experienced a serious problem with team selection. Whenever there was a match against King William's College scheduled, most of their team would come down with mysterious illnesses in the preceding week. The implication being that they wished to avoid our rather vigorous approach. The public school system always boasted of the stress it placed on good sportsmanship, 'It matters not who wins or loses - play up, play up and play the game etc.' If his recollections are correct, it would seem that we never quite took that sentiment on board.

This brief outline of my school record isn't just for the fun of things, it does have some relevance to the story. In the art class, the master was a Mr. Glover and he and I got along more as friends than as master and pupil. No, it wasn't like that, he was a good man and one of the very few masters who could have passed as normal in decent society. Despite my opinion that art is almost impossible to apply schoolroom type marks to, it was part of his job to do so and so he did, and as I say, I usually came at or near the top. However, I always assumed that this marking was more a question of him being polite to someone he got along with, than any intrinsic measure of my ability. Which was why I was unsurprised when subsequently, at full time art school, I found myself to be somewhere short of the top. I had gone from being a big fish in a small pond . . . you get it.

Where the excellent Mr. Glover, had a lasting effect on me was that he introduced me to a book; Batsford's, The Parish Churches of England. You see, we finally got there, I told you there was going to be a point to all this.

CHAPTER SIX

Leading to the Confessions of
a Counterfeit Christian

Mr. Glover's intention was to use this book as the basic textbook in our discussions on church architecture, and it was very useful as such; gothic tracery, linenfold panelling, hammer beam roofs and the great wool churches of East Anglia. But it was somewhat more than that for me. It awakened an interest not just in the structures themselves, but also their use and place in the community, and then the Reformation and the transfer of the buildings from the Church of Rome to the Church of England.

English parish churches are the key to an enormous part of England's social history and are, for me, a fascinating subject. My focus was originally on the architecture and the history, I came to the religion a little later.

So there you have it, the first of the excellent bad reasons for me being a Christian; I like the architecture. I have come to appreciate the sense of sanctity in such buildings and the historical continuity. When participating in a service in my own parish church in Cheshire, I am taking part in a continuous pattern of celebration and worship that has been enacted on that site for more than a thousand years. It is impossible to do this without a sense of belonging to something far bigger and more lasting than my own small self.

Why on earth would I wish to revisit the Hermitage, the Tower of London, the Sydney Opera House or the Duomo in Florence, when a mile down the road is one of the most beautiful buildings I have ever set eyes on? And it's still alive and doing exactly what it was built for. A building in which I am made welcome and am part of its community.

A minor incidental feature, one of many that you find in such buildings, is the presence of memorial plaques on the walls. One of them records the death of a certain Colonel Stanley Rimmer with the words, '. . . who perfected the tale of his days on New Year's Eve 1944. He feared God: Served his King: Loved his fellow men.' You could be dismissive and say that in strictly literary terms such an expression is formulaic, and maybe it is - but it gets me. As long as that plaque stands, Stanley, whoever he was, is in some sense, still with us.

All of which proves that I'm a sucker for high quality architecture and a bit of traditionalist, but does it prove anything else? A reasonable question might be: would I still go to church if it was in an undistinguished 1950's suburban building, with a fading sign outside saying, *'CH--CH, What's Missing? UR!'*? I would like to say yes, but honestly my heart sinks at the prospect, and that doesn't sound very dedicated, does it? One wonders at the genuineness of my Christian commitment.

Church music and hymns are next. I have heard hymns in general described as trite, banal, devoid of meaning and no better than football chants. I have personally encountered hymns that don't scan, and some that don't fit their musical setting. Others are just plain hopeless and were probably stolen from William Topaz McGonagall's reject pile. Then there's that tune for Deutschland, Deutschland Uber Alles, which comes up with some hymns, and it can be difficult to keep your right arm by your side. And yes, All Things Bright and Beautiful does prompt the gag reflex.

But, but, but, but, but, when you've got rid of that lot, there are still plenty left. Hymns that inspire, console and just make you smile; hymns that it's impossible not be uplifted by. That's why they're so popular, that's why they've lasted so long. There is also the inestimable advantage to singing hymns in church, no one can possibly object to your musicality, or lack thereof. You give it your best shot and however it turns out is fine, absolutely fine.

There are lots of hymns that I enjoy singing and from which I derive pleasure on several levels, but any list that I give of personal favourites would probably annoy as many people as it pleased. Try to remember the last time you went round to someone's house for a meal, someone you like and whose judgement you would normally trust, and they were playing background music. Can you honestly tell me you've never asked yourself, 'Gordon Bennett - are they strangling the cat?'

But I'll offer a few hostages to fortune by telling you what has come up on my i-Tunes list of recently repeated hymns. How Great Thou Art, in Welsh, Lo He Comes With Clouds Descending, The Angel Gabriel and finally The Day Thou Gavest, sung by the Wallingford Parish Church Choir. No, I don't know where Wallingford is either - who cares? But I do plan to go there one day. In fact if you can listen to that last one with a stony face then you probably died last week, but you're so dumb you haven't worked it out yet.

Then we have the liturgy, the actual format of the service. No matter which service; Matins, Communion or Evensong. I find reassurance and meaning in all of them, though the one I most frequently attend is Communion. But here we come to a major difficulty in trying to describe just how much of a committed Christian I am. Having a lifetime's familiarity with the King James' version of the bible and Cranmer's Book of Common Prayer; I sometimes have difficulty deciding if my love of the words is primarily a love of the poetry and the precision of the language, or if it's my sympathy and connection with the integral meaning.

The answer is that the feelings are mixed, and at times I'm unsure which predominates. Cranmer's rendering of the General Confession, of the Bendictus and of the Magnificat would still move me if I had no religious faith whatever, and more significantly might even cause me to ask myself *why* I had no faith, if this was how it was expressed.

What I know for sure is that, despite agreeing unconditionally that the conduct of the service should be in the local vernacular, if it's not understood in the pews - it's pointless, I have for most of my life been accustomed to Cranmer's Book of Common Prayer. Those are the words whose combination of poetry and meaning captured and convinced me. I grew up with those words and they will be imprinted on my mind until dementia or death remove me. Most of the services I now attend use the modern translation of the New Revised Standard Version, so I've adapted and am happy with that; but sometimes I still secretly grieve at the loss of the habitual and reassuring phrases that I grew up with.

In physics there is something called the Observer Effect which, as I understand it, when applied to quantum mechanics, shows that certain systems or particles cannot be observed without the observation itself distorting the subject. My own religious beliefs exhibit a similar unhelpful property. They exist and can be seen to do so by their effect on my life and thought processes. Unfortunately, the closer and more detailed any scrutiny of them becomes, the less clear is the outcome.

It would be convenient if this were not so, but I cannot avoid the fact that, to a third party, some aspects of my beliefs might seem to be mutually incompatible. An example might be my supposedly mainstream Christian standpoint, when set alongside my comments in this book on charity and prayer. If there are inconsistencies here, then I shall just have to accept them.

*****

There are the less obvious, but still very real feelings that surround religious observance in any society and although we might wish to deny it, these can often influence our own approach. Attitudes to religion will naturally vary from country to country, but as Britain is where I live, then those are the attitudes I refer to. You might ask yourself; do my friends go to church, and if not, how will I explain to them why I have suddenly started to do so? It can be awkward and embarrassing to raise religion in a largely agnostic and materialist society.

In some circles it can be socially less acceptable to say you believe in God than to tell them your name is on the Sex Offender's Register, and that wasn't meant as a joke.

Amongst those to whom this applies, I imagine the effect to be greatest in the young, by which I mean those less than middle aged. I'm in my sixties and by that age a lot of us have developed a thick enough skin to shrug off anyone else's raised eyebrows or sarcasm, to feel that we don't really care what other people think. It's a question of being sufficiently confident of your own judgement, of not needing other people to validate your choices.

The Financial Times recently ran a suicidally bad advertising campaign, to suggest that if you didn't read their newspaper you didn't know what to think. The strap line was, 'No FT - No Opinion!' Which made it sound as though all their readers were desperately insecure; and one can sometimes get the same feeling about the more evangelical atheists.

At rite of passage services, such as Christenings and weddings, you will occasionally see members of the congregation, obliged to be present for family reasons, who are not just uncomfortable to be there, but want to let you know about it. They are almost always men, women tend to be more pragmatic about life's little irritations, and such people usually communicate this discomfort by their posture. Typically, one hand stuffed in a trouser pocket and a sort of passive aggressive slouch, 'You're not fooling me with your mumbo jumbo'.

As a Church Warden I sometimes felt an unfulfilled urge to go over and say, 'Look we're only going to be another half hour, but if you're feeling *that* self-conscious then why don't you just go outside, sit on a tombstone and play with yourself.' But, being typically English, I thought it rather than saying it.

With such people and their millions of less demonstrative sympathisers in mind, is there any possibility that a belief in God can sometimes be reinforced by a contrarian desire to do that which might surprise or disturb those around us? Rather like declaring an intention of voting Liberal Democrat, or leaving your wife of forty years to go off with an Egyptian belly dancer. There's that delightful French phrase that has some relevance here, *épater la bourgeoisie,* or very loosely, to smack the complacent.

Of course I don't think these motives apply to me, in the same way that none of us believes that we're influenced by advertising; but then it's notoriously difficult to analyse your own motives and behavioural prompts.

For me, these are all contributory elements to my Christian faith, even some of the ones like architecture, which really shouldn't have such an effect. They act cumulatively, helping to tip the balance in a particular direction. But for me, there's one thing above all else that makes the final difference, that decides the issue. That is the fact that Christianity is a religion of the word. The opening of John's Gospel: 'In the beginning was the word, and the word was with God, and the word was God.' Which you could say brings me back to the poetry, and why not?

This is a very personal response and it might not have anything like the same relevance to anyone else, but through the years I have derived so much benefit from the words of the Book of Common Prayer that I find it difficult to imagine a life without it.

At this point I could start to list the passages of scripture that have from time to time affected me, moved me, amused me, inspired me and even seriously annoyed me, but I don't wish to offer a suggested reading list because, as with music, my choices won't be yours. These are things you have to select for yourself, and even then they can vary with your mood on the day.

However, a great many people now learn nothing of the bible or the prayer book at school and never go near a church. Any such person looking for a starting point, somewhere to dip an experimental toe in the water, could do worse than Paul's first letter to the Corinthians, chapter 13, it's a very well known piece. In the modern version it's the chapter that starts;

'If I speak in the tongues of mortals and of angels, but do not have love, I am a noisy gong or a clanging cymbal.' Quite interestingly, further on in that chapter it continues, *'For now we see in a mirror, dimly, but then we will see face to face. Now I know only in part; then I will know fully, even as I have been fully known.'* Which is not a million miles from my view of evolutionary theory. (This is the section that the King James' version gives as, 'For now we see through a glass darkly . . .' But if reading the King James' version, remember that what they call 'charity' is what we now call 'love'.)

Just one more biblical quote, and it's a relatively short one. If pressed to give a brief statement of their faith a lot of Christians might choose one of the two well known creeds, the Apostles' or the Nicene; 'I believe in one God . . etc.' But I would go for something even simpler than that, in fact the piece in question is more of an instruction manual than a statement of faith, but then perhaps instruction is what I'm most in need of. Psalm 100, often known by its Latin title, Jubilate Deo, is usually included in Anglican Morning Prayer; this is Cranmer's version:

O be joyful in the Lord all ye lands: serve the Lord with gladness, and come before his presence with a song.

Be ye sure that the Lord he is God: it is he that hath made us, and not we ourselves: we are his people and the sheep of his pasture.

O go your way into his gates with thanksgiving, and into his courts with praise: be thankful unto him, and speak good of his name.

For the Lord is gracious, his mercy is everlasting: and his truth endureth from generation to generation.'

For me that pretty much sums it up, and I'm happy to rest on that as an expression of my faith. If by chance, there's anyone out there who still thinks that was written by a monkey, even a highly developed and very sophisticated monkey, even a monkey on steroids, then I think it's time for the men in white coats. What do you think?

Before moving on to a slightly different area, there's one thing you can do with someone who has a religious faith that you can't do with an atheist, and it is to ask them this question. 'Would you still hold your current beliefs had you been born and raised in a completely different culture?'

Theoretically, this should offer some clue as to how carefully thought out their religious beliefs are. I've tried it on myself. Clearly, had I found myself to be the product of a different culture I would have been, in many ways, a different person. Yet there would still have been an essential personality that was recognisably me, in any society. I think that my core values would still have been present.

Had I been born into Greek or Russian Orthodoxy, that would have presented me with no problems. Neither would being born into Roman Catholicism, I would have coped with the multitude of saints, even with the Pope and transubstantiation. To be honest I'm half way there already. Being born into Judaism, Christianity's forerunner, could also have fitted my natural sympathies and instincts. As for Sikhism, Buddhism or Hinduism, I must, shamefacedly, confess that I don't know enough about them to offer a meaningful answer. But when it comes to Islam, then I think I would have had trouble.

Even finding that I had been born and raised a Muslim might not have been enough to overcome my repugnance at their views on women and their treatment of apostates. If your religion cannot accept the possibility that someone might no longer wish to be a member, then you're on the wrong side of a very important line between tolerance and intolerance.

As for the long accepted, though now disputed question, of the way that Islam was, or was not, spread by the sword. The daily newspapers throughout my adult life, and especially recently, seem to have provided their own running commentary on that story, and it's not a commentary I would feel comfortable to have representing my beliefs.

Then again, perhaps my opening assumption was wrong, perhaps you *can* ask an atheist that question about still holding your beliefs in a different society and culture. Consider; how many insistent atheists would be facing Mecca and praying five times a day, if they knew the alternative was death? I suggest the answer would be most of them, traditionally it has been religious people who were prepared to die for their beliefs. All I have to do now is to work out if that is a good thing.

Going back over the earlier parts of this account, I see that I have frequently used references to reading or writing poetry as a metaphor for civilisation or spirituality, and I have no wish to change that. However, I am concerned that you might take these references as subliminal suggestions to the effect that I'm a very cultivated sort of person, and have seriously high brow tastes. Oh dear. To set the record straight, I am a retired ship's chandler with a rackety background, who is now a registered firearms dealer and occasionally drinks too much. The only reason I write prose is because I can't write poetry, any whiff of aesthetic pretension should be met with hollow laughter and a slow hand clap as I leave the room.

CHAPTER SEVEN

Certain Matters of Morality

Regarding my character and moral standing. Other than what is already implicit in the text, I wasn't sure if I was going to cover that area, and I'm still not completely convinced it's a good idea. But having covered so many other influences from my past I suppose it would be cowardly to avoid the subject, and it might have some bearing on what you think of the facts and ideas that I've presented. Or, come to that, what you think of me.

My last book, a fictional autobiography of Barabbas, helpfully entitled - 'Barabbas', under the name Ian Lindsay, began with him looking back over his life and remarking what an unpleasant person he had once been, and might still be. That comment, like so much in my books was a genuine personal feeling of my own. I'm not eaten up by guilt over any of my past actions, not even remotely: which I suppose is a question in itself, but I do acknowledge that so many times when I say that someone else's behaviour is unacceptable I have actions of my own that are as bad or worse.

I can't imagine why you should, but were you ever to look, then I'm afraid you wouldn't find very much moral high ground under my feet.

A fact that I hadn't previously noticed, seems to be prompted by that remark in the last paragraph, about my fictional characters' actions reflecting my own feelings. As well as in Barabbas, in my five adventures published under my own name, all the lead characters share one particular personality trait. It is the regrettable willingness to kill anyone who gets in their way, with remarkably little compunction.

In case anyone else has noticed this, I have now, for the first time, wondered if that also reflects something of myself. I don't know who I'm quoting and don't really care, but the appropriate phrase would seem to be; that nothing human is alien to me. So could I, as a private individual in civilian life, kill someone?

Given the right set of highly improbable and extreme circumstances then I suppose that, just like you, if you're honest about it, I could. I think that anyone who says they could never kill another human being under any circumstances, must have a very limited and dull imagination, and no family. (You can choose that to mean either that you might occasionally wish to kill some member of your own extended family, or to take revenge on anyone who beat you to it.)

Perhaps we should simply both be grateful that the requisite circumstances are so extreme and improbable that they haven't yet come to pass. Naturally, I speak mainly for myself - I don't know about you. In that particular case, what I show in the books really is fiction - and likely to stay that way.

During the earlier brief account of my school days, I mentioned shoplifting amongst my other accomplishments, and if the subject is to be raised at all it might be better to avoid the term shoplifting, it's far too euphemistic. The correct description is, that between the ages of about eleven and thirteen, I was an occasional thief. Where did you think those four volumes of Sholokhov's work, and all the other books that I was busy reading, came from? Even worse, I suspect the reason for me eventually abandoning theft was not moral, but simply the fact that my income from the horses, and some small scale buying and selling, was sufficient to cover my outgoings.

Some years later I looked for the book shops in question, with a view to repaying the money, but they were long gone; I only hope it wasn't me that drove them over the edge, but I certainly can't have helped. Perhaps the worst part of this is that the closest I can get to feeling guilty is a vague and mild regret accompanied by a mental shrug.

When we get to the harder stuff in my schooldays, it isn't illegality that was the problem - that's never really troubled me, but indifference. And I don't mean my indifference to illegality, but my indifference to the examples of unpleasantness I saw around me. Which is more significant than it sounds.

I mentioned that my school was fairly brutal, and it was, and that included some degree of bullying. I was never a bully myself and was never the victim of bullying, but I did see it going on. There were some boys whose lives were made a daily misery, not so much by gross physical assault, though that did occur, as by a constant drip feed of casual abuse and denigration, and by a failure to include them in any activity.

You can say that the masters should have spotted this and taken action, you can say that the parents should have seen the unhappiness and done something, and they should; but they were at one remove. The people who witnessed it at first hand were the uninvolved fellow pupils standing round the edges of these events, and I was one of them.

I was large enough, aggressive enough and sufficiently aware, that I could have taken effective steps to prevent a great deal of the bullying that took place anywhere near me, and yet I didn't. I couldn't be bothered to get involved, I chose to walk by on the other side of the road as it were, I was nobody's Good Samaritan. I was one of the people who knowingly allowed such activities to continue. Some of the victims must still be suffering the effects of this treatment today, going through your schooldays as a constant victim must leave permanent scars.

My inaction is something that I still regret and always will. And this regret can show itself in unexpected ways. About ten years ago, one of my daughters ran a high street store and I occasionally helped her out (I have this uncanny knack for spotting shoplifters). One day I saw a woman casually watching as two of her teenage children taunted a Down's Syndrome man in one of the aisles, I told them to leave him alone. The children told me to 'eff off' and the mother rounded on me, saying it was none of my business, and anyway 'people like him' shouldn't be mixing with decent normal people.

My reaction had nothing to do with the nobility of my cause, or the quest for natural justice, I just knew that I had idly averted my gaze from this scenario once too often and thus went off at the deep end. I called her an 'ugly lard arsed bitch', she was slightly overweight, and threatened to disfigure her and her two 'subnormal brats'. When they'd gone, threatening to report me to the police, head office, Trading Standards, a solicitor, the

General Moderator of the Church of Scotland and anyone else they could think of, Sarah, my daughter, called out, 'Somebody needs to make my dad a cup of tea.'

As a minor aside to the last paragraph, when the woman and her odious children had left, the shop staff all burst into applause, and what's interesting is why. They weren't applauding me, or the fact that I had put stop to anti social behaviour; they were applauding the fact that a loud and unpleasant customer had been publically humiliated. A thing they so often wished to do themselves.

Unless you have actually worked in a shop yourself, you will probably never understand just how deeply some shop staff can hate their less pleasant customers.

Moving on from my schooldays, as a young man I spent just over a year working for another company, it's the only time in my life that I haven't worked for myself.

Having decided that my artistic skill was more suited to designing the stripes on pyjama trousers than earning a living, I had left art school and after a year or so spent doing nothing very much, had emigrated to Bergen in western Norway.

My main motive was to avoid joining the family ships chandler's business, and Norway was a country I had fond memories of, as we had spent several long family summer holidays in the south of that country when I was a child. It was also just about far enough from Liverpool for me to feel safe from family recruitment.

My father had had some connection with Norway during the war, having been for a while a British Intelligence liaison with what was called the Shetland

Bus operation. This was the clandestine use of fishing boats between German occupied Norway and the UK for the movement of agents and arms. The name of the operation was sarcastically derived from the frequency and regularity of this covert and highly dangerous service. Before I left England he had given me the benefit of his local knowledge,

'There are only two occupations on the Norwegian coast, fishing and fornication, and there's no fishing in winter.' (One of those words is quite close to the one he used.)

Mindful of my father's timetable, I left England in the late Autumn of 1965, with my worldly goods, my hopes for the future and some spare socks, all packed into an old Mini.

At Tyne Commission Quay in North Shields, the car was hoisted aboard a Bergen Line steamer, there wasn't enough vehicular traffic to justify a roll on roll off ship on that route. Only the most eccentric travellers took their cars to the west coast of Norway. Once you were out of Bergen itself, the road system was usually gravel and often no more than a pot holed single track, and even then interrupted at regular intervals by the need to take yet another ferry across the next fjord.

Two days later I was deposited onto the rain swept dockside of Norway's second city, the inhabitants of which seemed to have made absolutely no preparations for my arrival; no mayor, no bands, no bunting. Quite frankly, it was a bit of a let down.

After spending a few nights in a cheap flop house I found myself accommodation, and obtained work with the supply department of a large local company who were variously; ship owners, hotel owners and transport contractors.

To start with I was a warehouse lad and acted as second man on one of the delivery trucks, an undemanding role with few responsibilities, which was fine as it allowed me time to work my way through a book called Teach Yourself Norwegian in Seven Weeks. It was a slim volume, so I simply learned the whole book off by heart, and then did my best to translate the front page of the local newspaper with a dictionary every night. Happily, this was before the days of serious North Sea Oil development, and so none of the people I mixed with spoke much English. This left me with no option but to learn their language, or forever keep my mouth shut, it wasn't a difficult decision.

Getting to grips with the language, I was delighted to find that it had a very straightforward grammatical system, with a similar sentence construction to English. It was probably a good deal easier than learning German, and a million miles easier than Finnish, which I think is close to impossible.

While I was living in Bergen the Beatles released a track called 'We All Live in a Yellow Submarine'. I not only had to translate every word of the lyrics for the people at work, I had to make it scan so they could sing along with it, but in Norwegian. Pop song lyrics really don't bear such close examination, but it was probably a useful exercise.

Although any Norwegian language skills have long since atrophied through lack of use, one or two pearls remain. In the knowledge that *himmel* means heaven, *fart* can mean either speed or travel and *dag* means day, it will come as no surprise to learn that the Norwegian for Ascension Day is *Kristi Himmelfartsdag.* I always found this to be more pleasingly graphic than the English version.

One day, we arrived back at the warehouse after delivering supplies to one of their hotels in town, to find the splendidly remote figure of Mr. Olsen, the general manager, his nervous clipboard carrying assistant and the senior supply department foreman, waiting for us on the loading bay.

Pedersen, the driver, and I were told to wait on one side, while the assembled big cheeses searched the vehicle. They must have had a tip off, because behind the driver's seat they unearthed a large block of frozen reindeer meat, an expensive luxury item. The driver was fired on the spot and I was told to go home.

Arriving the next morning at my normal start time of six thirty, I was told to wait in the canteen until Olsen arrived at nine and then report to his office. It was a long walk from the basement supply department at the back of the building, up to the ground floor and through two or three other departments, to the front of the building, and the manager's office. It seemed as though the people in each department I passed through knew what was going on.

'You heard about what happened last night - well that's the English bloke, on his way to see Olsen.' This was followed by pursed lips and a sharp intake of breath.

After my long wait in the canteen, I had convinced myself that they were going to try and pin some of the blame on me, if you're looking for a fall guy then a young immigrant with no connections is an easy target.

As I made my way through the building I had managed to work myself into a high level of self righteous indignation. My actual involvement in the theft was limited to a serious annoyance at *not* having been involved, and an absolute certainty that I could have organised things better, and not been caught. I'd had the benefit of a decent education that covered exactly this sort of area, I knew how these things were done.

By the time I arrived at Olsen's office I was determined to involve the British Embassy in Oslo, and probably the Ambassador himself. They might take me down, but it wouldn't be a free ride - I was going to hurt someone on the way.

I knocked and was told to enter, and was then treated to the routine which involves you standing there like a spare part, while the man behind the desk finishes writing War and Peace, without acknowledging you.

Eventually he did, and I was ready for him. Just one wrong word and he could shove his job, he could shove his company and he could shove the rest of Bergen with it, I wasn't going to be blamed for somebody else's shenanigans, especially when they were as badly organised as this.

Eventually he gave me his attention, he stared at me for a while, and then asked,

'Can you drive?'

I stared back at him, this was not what I'd expected, so I narrowed my eyes and tried to work out what was going on. Before I came up with an answer he asked again, louder and slower, for the foreigner,

'Can - you - drive?' By this time I'd worked out the correct response.

'Of course I can drive, I've got my own car.' He breathed deeply and spoke even more slowly,

'No, I don't mean a car; can you drive a truck?' By now I was beginning to get the idea.

'Yes.'

'Right then, when we're busy I want you to cover part of Pedersen's job.'

He looked relieved to have settled the matter, waved his hand dismissively, returned his attention to the paperwork and carried on writing. I thought for a moment,

'But I don't have a Norwegian commercial driving licence, what do I say if the police stop me?'

'Just tell them to speak to me.' He said, without looking up. I carried on standing there, I was sure there was something else we needed to cover.

Finally he looked back at me, raised his wrist and tapped his watch. 'It's now twenty past nine, you should have started work nearly three hours ago.'

I turned to leave, but with my hand on the door I finally remembered what the other thing was. I thought it probably came under the heading of pushing my luck, but went for it anyway.

'If I'm doing Pedersen's job, that must mean I'm getting Pedersen's wage.'

He grunted, tapped the end of his pen on the desk for a while and then sighed. 'Very well - now get out of here, I'm busy.'

Always liking to make sure of these things, I thought that I'd stop off in the payroll department on the way back.

'Olsen says that I'm to get a pay rise, to whatever Pedersen was on.'

The young woman looked at me, puzzled and slightly surprised, but said nothing, so I persevered.

'It's just that I'm doing Pederson's job now, so I'm to get the same pay.'

At last she spoke. 'Yes, we know all about that, he told us last night.' and then carried on looking puzzled, still wondering why I was there. It was one of those moments when you think; I don't know why I bother.

After I had become familiar with the new arrangement for a few weeks the foreman of an adjoining department invited me in for a little chat. After some general nonsense about how deep the snow was and the price of tea in China, or whatever, he came to the point. He said that some unspecified friends of his had noticed how well I was settling in, and thought that I was the sort of person who might like to take on some extra responsibility, and help them out from time to time.

'Nothing major, you understand, just moving the odd few boxes here and there, whilst you're out on other jobs, and of course you'll be paid for it.'

I wasn't too happy to have been so easily spotted as a crook, I would have hoped to have been more discreet and subtle, but that's never been my forte. Anyway, the man in question was a likeable, softly spoken man in his sixties, and my impression was that, unlike Pedersen, this was a man who could organise *this sort of thing* properly.

Nothing was ever put into direct and vulgar words about the possible content of these boxes, and I knew better than to ask. In fact if you'd read a transcript of the conversation you wouldn't have seen reference to any sort of criminal activity, but face to face there was no doubt that whatever was involved, it wouldn't bear any sort of official scrutiny. It was a nod and a wink sort of conversation, but no less clear for that.

Would I have done this in England? It makes no sense to say it, and I know it sounds stupid, but it would have seemed somehow more serious and more illegal in England. There was a feeling that when in Bergen I was on tour, and what happens on tour stays on tour.

At all events this turned into a regular arrangement. I would be given instructions about an address, or more frequently a shed on the docks, to go to, where I would find anything from five to fifty boxes. The organisation was sufficiently tight that I never encountered anyone with the goods, although I always assumed that someone would be keeping an eye on them. I would load the boxes myself, throw a tarpaulin over them and then simply drive away.

There was never any problem with the dock gate police, but whether this was because they'd been fixed or because I was lucky I don't know. You need to be either lucky, or stupid, to take that sort of risk without worrying, perhaps I was both.

I would then deliver them to another address, or meet a designated vehicle in a car park somewhere and transfer them. Where identifiable, the goods in question were almost always spirits; whisky, gin, vodka, brandy and such like, and there was never any attempt to deny the fact that they were stolen or more probably smuggled goods, I took it for granted that I handled both.

Hard drugs weren't the problem in the mid sixties that they later became, so the problem of whether I would or wouldn't handle them never arose. However, as there wasn't the widespread awareness of the effects of drug addiction in those days, then I can't honestly claim it would have been a major sticking point.

From a long established mixture of social and religious reasons, Norwegian legislation at that time strictly controlled the importation, distribution and sale of wines and spirits. In fact the availability of all alcohol, except for low strength beer, was extremely restrictive, with some towns on the coast being completely dry.

The only legal sales of wine and spirits were through a state run chain of outlets called

Vinmonopolet, these places were so bureaucratic and gloomy that if you didn't need a drink when you went in, you would by the time you came out. I've forgotten the precise amounts, but there was a strictly applied ration of how much each person could buy in any period.

Just as with Prohibition in America it was a system that was guaranteed to lead to bootlegging and smuggling, and it did. The continuing fact that so many parliaments pass so many laws which directly increase the amount of crime on the streets, has always been one of life's curiosities.

It was apparent that Pedersen's offence hadn't been the dishonesty, which was considered a minor matter, so much as the fact that it was unsanctioned dishonesty, which is a horse of a very different colour. Instead of working through the proper channels he'd been trying a little private enterprise, somebody hadn't liked that and he'd been shopped.

It is no coincidence, that even whilst I was there, the most famous book in Norway was still a pre war book by a reformed criminal, Arthur Omre, called 'Smuglere', (Smugglers). They might not wear horned helmets any more, but as the Germans found out in the war, their coastline is pretty much uncontrollable, and they have a firm attachment to free market economics.

I don't wish to exaggerate my role in all of this, I was never anything more than a very small and junior cog in a larger organisation, and never knew or met anyone other than my immediate contacts. Even so I must admit that, whilst I never hit anyone over the head with a cosh myself, it is in the nature of things that organisations engaged in seriously criminal activity sometimes employ people who do. I was aware of all this at the time and untroubled by it, and took the payment offered without qualms.

So untroubled, in fact, that I was later happy to use a dramatised version of these experiences as the basis of my first full length, though unpublished, book. These are unedifying admissions, but as newspaper columnists say; all life is copy.

No matter how worldly wise I might have been as a bootlegger, I remained rather naive in other areas. One Friday that summer, the foreman refused my offer to work overtime on the Saturday afternoon, on the grounds that I was English. I became predictably annoyed and mildly abusive at this racial discrimination, but he made calm down gestures with his hands and said, 'I just meant that you'll be watching the match.'

To which I responded, 'What match?' I knew of no match.

This caused a degree of surprise and the other staff all stared at me.

'England are playing Germany and you can't miss that.' He explained, and then realising that not only had I not heard about the match, but that I didn't have a television set either, told me to come round to his house to watch it with him and his friends.

Even to this day, that remains the only football match I have ever seen, still I suppose that if there's only going to be one of them, the 1966 World Cup Final is probably a good choice.

I can't claim to have had suffered any subsequent pangs of remorse about my behaviour in Norway. If ever I find myself thinking about those days, it's usually along the lines of: it was all a long time ago and in another country, so frankly my dear, I don't give a damn.

I agree this is morally unacceptable and in this case, unlike the book stealing, I can't honestly manage even a vague and mild regret. However, apart from the money, there was one useful thing I did bring home with me from Norway. That was the ability to hand roll a cigarette with one hand, along the top of my leg, whilst simultaneously driving a truck with the other hand. And that's a thing you don't see too often.

CHAPTER EIGHT

Family Planning for Beginners

I don't think that my reluctance to endorse abortion as a method of birth control is based on my religious views, I certainly don't support it with scriptural texts or theological points. To me, my extremely strong reservations about abortion seem to be based as much on humanist as religious principles, they feel like a natural human concern for the sanctity of life.

You don't need to believe in any sort of God to think that killing babies, even unborn ones, is generally a bad idea. I agree that there can be exceptional circumstances where abortion is called for, I'm not going to list them, you can work them out for yourself; sufficient to say that such circumstances can exist. But that's the whole point about exceptional circumstances, they are exceptional, not routine.

No matter what the law says, or what safeguards are supposed to be in place; the real life position in Britain today, is that any woman can abort any child for any reason. That wasn't always the case.

I wouldn't want to live in a society that tried to equate morality with legality, you only have to look at some of the places that have seriously tried it; Florence under Savonarola and Cambodia under Pol Pot. One approached the fight against immorality from a religious standpoint and the other from a political, both of them mad as hatters and both willing to kill as many people as it took to achieve their own standards of 'purity'.

But if you rule out such extremity there is still an undeniable area where morality must inform and guide the law. While this morality has most often been religious it doesn't have to be, the point is that law making needs to be based on some moral consensus; killing people is bad just because it is, you don't need any further discussion. If we say that the foetus, at some stage of its development, should be regarded as an unborn child, rather than an inconsequential blob of mucus, then killing it involves more than just the mother's interests. (The fact that the appropriate verb in that sentence was 'killing' rather gives the game away.) At that point I think we've reached the area where morality and the law meet.

When I was about nineteen, my then girlfriend announced that she was pregnant, her monthly cycle was regular and entirely predictable, if her period was late it was time to start worrying. After three weeks of no show, she said that her body felt different and that she was sure she was pregnant. The pregnancy was unplanned and unwanted, but we could have coped, I offered to marry her but she didn't think my heart was in it, and I think she was right.

By present standards my offer of marriage sounds incredibly Victorian, and no doubt you could say that any marriage built on those foundations would be doomed to fail, and maybe you're right, but I wouldn't bank on it. Anyway, going back to 'then'.

112

The law at that time prohibited abortion in all but the most extreme and unmistakeable medical emergencies, and my views on the subject were much the same then as now. I thought casual abortion, for reasons of convenience was seriously immoral. But that was when it involved other people's convenience, now, for the first time, it involved my own convenience and my girlfriend's convenience, and that was different.

Without so much as a moral blink, and with no concern for the law, I made contact with a local midwife, who, I was told could arrange these things, and we agreed a price. I don't know why people talk about back street abortionists, as though they were all seedy and disreputable old crones, refugees from Macbeth, this one wasn't. She was a pleasantly spoken middle aged woman with a wholly professional attitude, and a very civilised approach.

Then a day or two later, before the planned abortion had been performed, my girlfriend's period arrived; panic over. She had simply missed an entire month, how or why I have no idea, but it happened.

What this episode did reveal was the extremely shaky foundations my morals rest on, at the slightest threat to my own interests, or in fairness the interests of those close to me, my morals collapse like a house of cards and I start making other arrangements. That old phrase; Lack of Moral Fibre seems to be floating around here.

*****

Margaret and I were married in 1974, we were both in our twenties, both fit and healthy and both wanted children, there was no reason to think there would be any delay. But nothing happened, and so after a while we saw the doctor, who told us to stop panicking and just get on with things. After two years we began to insist and were referred to specialists, we were both examined, prodded and tested and still nothing happened. Doctors assured us that two or three years was nothing in such matters and there would only be cause for concern after five or ten years, I thought that was nonsense and wanted something to happen now, or at least a lot faster than five or ten years.

By this time it was coming up to the three year mark and we had both begun to accept that it might never happen, though we were unsure where to go next. We had seen other childless couples turn into professional baby hunters, devoting their whole lives to the search for fertility and we had no intention of going down that route.

I might not be very spiritual but I am fairly resourceful, and I thought that I could see a possible Plan B. In order to understand how and why this came about, you need to appreciate that in the late 1970s in Britain the adoption services were in the grip of a manic fever of political correctness, it was almost Maoist in its intensity. It was taken as matter of indisputable fact that the traditional family unit; mother, father and children was a paternalist middle class conspiracy against the interests of the proletariat. It looks absurd even to write that down, but it was a fact.

As soon as you applied to register as potential adoptive parents you would be investigated by some radically indoctrinated young social worker, determined to sniff out your failings. These included: being a Christian (other religions were acceptable because they were considered *ethnic*), running your own business, having been to private school or just thought to be middle class, any one of which was enough to permanently disqualify you.

Questions would be asked of your political views and voting patterns, and worst of all if you dared to suggest that you might like to adopt a baby of the same racial type as yourselves, this would prove that you were racists and never to be allowed near a child of any sort.

Which, interestingly, is the exact opposite of the current insistence that racial types stay together; on the grounds that no white parent could possibly understand a black child's needs. These two implacable dogmas being equally outrageous. The interview process could, and very often did, drag on for several years with no guarantee of the outcome, or any possibility of appeal.

In case you think any of that last paragraph to be an exaggeration, remember that it is only very recently that Rotherham Council social services department removed foster children from a couple, on the grounds that the couple's affiliation to a legitimate UK political party was not the sort of politics they approved of. The couple weren't racist or extremist and the party in question part of the political mainstream, but the politicised staff of the social services department thought they had the right to insist that foster parents should be forced to vote in a way they found acceptable. Even when the entirely unsurprising storm of outrage broke, so deeply seated was the departmental bigotry that nobody was disciplined, nobody apologised and the decision was never reversed.

In our own case, we would have needed to be desperate to even consider subjecting ourselves to this sort of deeply offensive nonsense, and we weren't. But, as I say, I thought that I had identified a Plan B, an alternative approach.

As a ship's chandler my working day was spent talking to ship's Captains, Chief Engineers and Chief Stewards of every nationality. In the morning I might sit down with, in turn: Indians, Germans and Koreans, and in the afternoon; Chinese, Greeks and Egyptians, and a thousand similar variations. In these surroundings I was able to make enquiries about the possibilities of adopting in another country. This was before the days of well organised trans border adoptions, or of pop singers going to Africa to adopt a cute baby as a photo opportunity, this was before any of that existed, it was virgin territory.

I discovered there were a great many instances of informal adoptions taking place, lots of anecdotal stories of friends or relatives known to have transferred an unwanted baby from one family to another. But these were all within some sort of related community, none of them crossed borders. Until one day I was talking to the Captain of a Dutch ship, who casually asked,

'Well then why don't you just buy one?'

It was as though someone had switched the light on, why didn't we just buy one? I had no answer.

I mentioned none of this to Margaret, I decided to wait until I was much further down the line, and had something organised. The Captain gave me the name of someone who he thought might know someone, and that was enough to get me started. After passing through three or four different intermediaries, I finally obtained the name of a lawyer in the Dutch capital, The Hague. He turned out to be the someone I needed. It was never openly spoken of as a purchase, always the talk was of an adoption, but neither of us had any doubts about the precise nature of the transaction; he was proposing to sell and I was proposing to buy: a baby.

I assumed that he had undertaken such transactions with other British people before, as his price was quoted in a nice round number of pounds sterling, four thousand to be exact. Bear in mind that this was more than thirty years ago, when four thousand pounds represented an even more significant sum than it does today, it was the price of a decent car.

The money was to be paid half up front, and half immediately prior to collection. The baby, a white Caucasian child, certified to be disease free, would be delivered to a nursing home, somewhere in the Netherlands and would be available for us to visit and have medically examined for a period of forty eight hours, at which time we would either pay the second half and then collect, or turn it down and walk away. Oddly, I don't remember ever discussing any choice of the child's gender, I was more concerned about whether or not the paperwork was going to be legally watertight; as I might already have mentioned, I should have been an accountant. Satisfied that I had everything in place I told Margaret that I had solved our problem, and wasn't I clever?

She was horrified, said that it was an appalling suggestion and that we would have nothing to do with any such scheme. Where did I imagine the child had been stolen from? Well I thought it was just an unwanted baby, an informal adoption with less paperwork than normal. Derisive laughter.

In retrospect I'm astonished at my willingness to enter into such a disreputable and unmistakeably criminal scheme and would like to think that, even without Margaret's intervention, I would have probably seen sense before going through with it. But the truth is that I was all primed and ready to go, I really think I might have completed the deal unless stopped. If nothing else in my life that episode should always hold me back from wagging any sort of a finger, literal or metaphorical, at anyone else. Even the unsavoury political bent of Rotherham Council looks fairly anodyne in comparison.

However, although not wishing to airbrush my own attempts at serious and criminal immorality, I still think that most of the pain in this world is caused by everyday small scale acts of envy, greed, malice and an unwillingness to get involved; mostly by people who will never be convicted of any wrongdoing. This is why I have always regretted my failure to stop the bullying I saw around me at school, far, far more than any concern over my juvenile shoplifting, or handling stolen goods and smuggling.

I don't regret the fact that I never objected to the persecution, prosecution, or just general taunting of homosexuals, Jews or black people, because it's currently fashionable to do so. I'm not a very fashionable person, and grew up in a time when such attitudes were not simply widespread, but socially acceptable. Surely it can't be a crime to simply go with the flow, can it? Well yes it can, especially if you're in a position to know better.

Remember, because of my job, I wasn't just the average man in the street who never knowingly met any of these categories. I met and worked with people from all sorts of racial groups, religious persuasions and colours, every day of the week. I cheerfully met them, talked with them, drank and ate with them and did business with them, so I should have known better; in fact the galling part of it is that I quite clearly *did* know better. Yet I still laughed at pub jokes about darkies, Pakkies and poofters, even when they weren't funny.

That's the bit that bothers me most, uncritically accepting other people's standards, when I had the ability to impose my own. Feebly following the pack, any pack at all, is always a far worse crime than racism, or any other politically defined *ism*.

In a continuation of my thoughts earlier in the book when I wondered if other people had experienced, if not similar examples of miracles to the ones I described, then shall we say parallel examples? My suspicion is that such experiences are much more widespread than might be thought, as so many people will rationalise these things away, not wanting to be seen as gullible.

In like manner, I take it for granted that my personal failings are not unique, they just happen to be the ones I'm most familiar with. Even my dabbling in criminality is comparatively low level, for all I know your own career as a serial bank robber, or contract killer, could leave me in the shade. Every adult human being has a back catalogue of crime, sin and malice, or for the less adventurous, perhaps, just occasional small minded nastiness. Even Mother Theresa must have wished ill to befall somebody sometime, in fact if you read some of her biographers it would seem that she did so quite regularly.

My point is that I don't think my experiences, or the conclusions I draw from them relate solely to me, I think I'm in good company, and even if you're not a bank robber, that probably still includes you.

It takes no courage or originality to say it, but it is nonetheless true that I never had any objections to same sex relationships, even when such objections were the norm. To parrot this opinion now is to do no more than conform to the views of all 'right thinking people';

whole hearted approval is de rigueur, and one wonders whether or not the activity should be made compulsory.

However, the fact is that I simply didn't care when I was younger, and still don't now; why would I be troubled by other peoples sexual couplings? I have enough trouble trying to sort out my own. There are a lot more interesting and noteworthy personal quirks about all of us than whether we go to bed with someone who does, or does not, (delete as applicable) possess a penis. Whether you are true to, and supportive of your partner, is infinitely more important than their gender. (You can embroider that last sentence into a framed sampler and hang it on your wall.)

The most unnatural thing about homosexuality is the Church of England's unhealthy fascination with this area. I regard biblical strictures on the subject as no more relevant than an injunction not to eat shellfish. As for Saint Paul's disapproval, he was certainly a man of God, but he was also a man of his time and he spoke as such, objecting to adultery and fornication in the same manner as homosexuality, and I'm only concerned about *them* for the collateral damage they cause and the depressing extent to which they normalise lying.

That last sentence is where the poison lies; the extent to which some particular behaviours *normalise lying*, and now that homosexuality has emerged into the daylight that leaves adultery as the most likely place to find it.

To the best of my knowledge the Church of England has never banned serial adulterers from being either bishops or vicars, their criterion seems to be that such behaviour should not be publically visible. As the Americans put it: don't ask and don't tell. Which makes our lengthy and public agonising over women and homosexual priests look strangely pointless.

Returning to me; in summary I get two out of ten, for my lack of effort and unwillingness to engage with the rest of the world. I have no illusions that my actions could have changed public attitudes, but I could have said something to protest about things that were said and done in front of me, and which I knew to be wrong. All that is necessary for the triumph of evil is that good men do nothing, and while I might not be a particularly good man I don't think I'm evil, but for quite a while, I certainly did nothing.

All this talk of my satisfaction with a multi racial working environment makes me sound uncomfortably modern and broad minded, and it's true that I did thoroughly enjoy mixing with such an assortment of nationalities and cultures. The odds and sods of the seven seas, and me. However, I'm happy to say that in the middle of all this sunshine and light I did manage to keep some small flames of irrational intolerance burning. I find it impossible to get on with the Japanese and don't like Swedes, and I'm not talking about turnips.

'But how can you possibly dislike a whole country, you silly little man?'

'The same way you get to Carnegie Hall – practise.'

I was brought up on stories of the Luftwaffe bombing England in aircraft that ran on Swedish ball bearings, that's my earliest memory of the use of the word profiteering. Then when I lived in Norway in the mid sixties, memories of the war were still strong and, counter intuitively, public feelings about the Swedes were even more negative than those about the Germans who had invaded and occupied their country. This was particularly so amongst the working class, which was the sea in which I swam.

It was said that the Swedish state railways had colluded with the Germans to move troops through Sweden to attack eastern Norway; it was also added, as an extra authenticating detail, that they hadn't even charged the Wehrmacht full fare but had granted them a special Group Discount. It's no good saying this story sounds improbable, that's beside the point, as in all such cases, the point is that the people telling it believed it was true.

A couple of years later I had spent a few days on business in Gothenburg in southern Sweden, and was then driving over to Stockholm. Half way there I suddenly realised that I had left my brand new electric razor, a red silk paisley pattern dressing gown (I was more of a fancy pants in those days) and the almost completed manuscript of a book, in a neat pile on the dressing table that morning.

I stopped at a log cabin cafe by a lake and rang back to the hotel in Gothenburg. The woman wasn't interested,

'There's none of your property here.'

'Look, I don't care about the brand new electric razor, or the red silk paisley pattern dressing gown, you can have them, All I want is the pile of papers that have no possible value to you.'

'Don't you tell me what we can or can't have - anything you left here is our property, now stop bothering me or I'll call the police.' Bang, the phone went down.

I began to understand the Norwegian view of their neighbours. Even today I still stop passing Swedes to ask if they've ever had a red silk paisley pattern dressing gown, but they've all lied about it.

*****

This recital of some of my more prominent failings has not been to unburden myself, my feelings of regret at elements of my behaviour might be genuine, but they don't keep me awake at night. I know I've taken a long time to get round to it, but what this whole chapter has been trying to do is to set the stage, and explain the background, to a very basic question about my religious beliefs.

That question being; is my interest in religion prompted by, and in response to, a desire to make amends for earlier behaviour. For good or ill, would I be what I am now, if I hadn't been what I was then?

Is it a re-run of my post operative treatment in intensive care; when they discovered I'd had no morphine for 36 hours and then tried to make up for this by giving me an overdose? Am I trying to do that with morality?

I've thought about it and If I knew the answer I'd tell you, unfortunately, the best I can come up with is that I really don't think so. But one point that did emerge from that consideration was the rather obvious fact that only sinners get religion.

Does that mean that a degree of satisfaction with your own behaviour is a component of atheism? I rather think it might - there's an awful stench of smugness to a lot of aggressive secularity.

Returning briefly to the subject of buying babies, we had just reached the point where Margaret had stopped me in my tracks. I think both of us were shocked at where the hunt had led, and decided it was time to change direction. So after considering our options we went to Manchester Airport and signed up for flying lessons, reckoning that if we weren't going to have children we could probably afford a plane instead.

No sooner had Margaret completed her Private Pilot's course than she found she was pregnant. And before you tell me, we've already heard every possible joke about the Mile High Club.

CHAPTER NINE

Paul and the Women

Having established that I am a traditional and mainly conformist member of the Church of England, might seem to be all there is to be said on the subject, however, as we're not even half way through the book, you can probably work out that's not the case. My trouble is that, even though I've settled myself semi comfortably into the welcoming embrace of the church, there are still a few pointed bits sticking in my ribs.

Before starting on that list I'll make some mention of the Apostle Paul. It's difficult to talk about Christianity without doing so. His letters, even most of those parts probably not written by him, are not just profound, they can also be extremely provocative, making it difficult to omit him from any list of New Testament subjects worth looking at more closely.

To do him any sort of serious justice would require another book on that subject alone, and there are already plenty of them on the market. Anyone seriously interested in a deeper study of Paul would be well advised to get themselves a copy of 'The Life and Epistles of St. Paul' by two eminent Victorian gentlemen, W.J. Conybeare and J.S. Howson. It looks a little heavy at first and the illustrations are pretty awful, but I promise you, to quote the Michelin Guide, it's worth a detour. It does, however, assume that its readers possess a higher level of education than I ever achieved. I quote one of the footnotes from page 65 of my own edition:

'It may be necessary to explain to some readers that the Greek imperfect merely denotes that the attempt was made . . .' May be necessary? Surely not.

With all that in mind I propose to do no more than give an expanded version of some of my own remarks about him, which appeared in an earlier book, and which seem to cover what I want to say here.

Paul's Epistles, his letters to the various new churches around the eastern Mediterranean, many of which were founded by him, are a fascinating source of information, both about the writer and the state of the early church. However, as they were written over a number of years, to different people, on different aspects of Christian life, it's not surprising that they contain some inconsistencies and anomalies. But to modern eyes the major interest always seems to be his supposedly anti feminine comments, which don't seem to match his actions.

The fact that some of the early churches that Paul either founded, or was in contact with, were led by women sits very uneasily with one or two of his high profile and frequently quoted comments about women. e.g. 'I do not permit a woman to teach or have authority over a man.' Yet in almost direct opposition to that is the lengthy description of marital equality to be found in First Corinthians chapter 7. A brief extract of which is: 'For the wife does not have authority over her own body, but the husband does; likewise the husband does not have authority over his own body, but the wife does.'

I expect that for a lot of people, including me, that's not what we expect to hear Paul saying about female equality, yet the remarks feel genuine and, unlike some of his other alleged comments, it serves nobody's agenda to have added them separately. Paul also writes, 'There is neither male nor female because Christ unites us.'

There is a serious difficulty in contrasting one part of his supposed sayings with another; and a further difficulty in contrasting those sayings with his actions. A sufficient difficulty to make one wonder if both positions came from the same man. Paul's strictures against female leadership are a genuine concern for the modern reader, especially when they are so clearly contradicted by his own actions. Yet if he didn't mean it - then why did he say it?

There are two obvious possible answers, the first being that perhaps he never did say some of the things attributed to him, perhaps the bigot was a later insertion by a different hand. I'm not a conspiracy theorist, the butler usually did it, the cock up view of history is almost always preferable to any sort of conspiracy. And yet, again and again I seem to return to the point that a degree of discernment needs to be employed when reading even the New Testament, the uncritical acceptance of every single phrase would be seriously misleading. A part of this book's purpose is to try and identify which those misleading passages are, and why.

I don't wish to be any more presumptuous than I already am - but if a passage of scripture looks and sounds like a cuckoo in the nest, then that, conceivably, is exactly what it is. As the Gershwin song puts it: 'The things that you're liable to read in the Bible, it ain't necessarily so.'

A second possible reason for him saying that he wished to restrict the role of women is one of political practicality. If you note his instruction that the new churches should avoid speaking in tongues, he nowhere claims this is because the practice itself is suspect, but simply that it is to be avoided because it will make outsiders think that church members are mad (his word, not mine).

Note also his instruction that the new churches should be respectful of local laws, customs and rulers. Once again this isn't because it will make them better Christians, but rather because it will enable them to go about their work without provoking unnecessary local antagonism. If you then come to his remarks about women not preaching you can see them as part of a continuum, respecting local traditions and ways, whether you agree with those ways or not.

Paul is saying: 'This might not be what I do - but these things will help you to preach the gospel unmolested.' Such an approach might not be the purest or most rigorously moral position imaginable, but when trying to preach the word of God to a hostile and uncaring first century audience, from a rigidly patriarchal background, it was intensely practical. And whatever else one might say about Paul, you have only to read his letters to see that he was an intensely practical man.

When writing about Mary Magdalen I was able to take a reasoned and reasonable guess about her appearance, but it was just guesswork, with Paul we have some actual clues to work with. One of the apocryphal gospels refers to him as short, bald and bow legged, and in Acts it says that the citizens of Lystra, looking at Paul and Barnabas together, instinctively assumed Barnabas to be the senior of the two, which suggests that Paul was not a physically imposing man. In further confirmation, when the people of Corinth met him for the first time, they commented that his appearance didn't live up to the power of his letters.

If this is true, and it sounds like it is, then it makes the strength of his personality all the more impressive. He was a man who swayed crowds, not by any physical presence, but by the force and passion of his arguments, by his sheer determination and personal belief.

One rarely mentioned fact about Paul, which might argue against his supposed misogyny, is that, unlike Jesus who only might have been married, Paul certainly was (as indeed was Simon Peter). As closely as we can calculate he was 31 years old at the time of his conversion on the road to Damascus, for an ambitious and orthodox Jew of that age to be unmarried would have been extremely unusual; unusual enough to have raised questions about just how orthodox he was.

Even more specifically, his election to the Sanhedrin, which can best be dated as coming after the death of Stephen and more than a year before his conversion, would have required not only that he be married, but that he should also be a father. While Paul states clearly in his first letter to the Corinthians that he was unmarried at the time he wrote that particular letter, it is not known whether he had been widowed by death or divorce, or when.

All of which leaves me feeling that while it's impossible to avoid mentioning him, my questions about Paul are more the subjects for discussion and rumination, than the occasion for argument or complaint. To go any more deeply into his life and writing would be to risk devoting the rest of this book to him, and I wish to spread my net a little more widely. For that reason I have restricted myself to this very brief mention of his supposed misogyny, and will now move on.

Which brings me to a short list of those aspects of Christian practice, or passages in the New Testament, which puzzle or trouble me. Things which I consider to be mistaken, implausible, or downright wrong, and if that doesn't sound arrogant for a retired ship's chandler, then nothing ever will.

CHAPTER TEN

Be Careful What You Pray For
– and a consideration of free will

I approach the next subject cautiously and with trepidation, I'm concerned, not only that I might be wrong, but that people I respect might find my views on this subject to be ill informed and offensive. I admit there is a real possibility that every one of my fellow congregation members, not to mention the Rector, might look at me askance and disagree with me. But this is a very personal book and I can't speak of how anyone else feels, I can only tell you how I feel.

The subject in question is prayer, and it's misuse. I am sure the bench of bishops will heave a massive and collective sigh of relief to hear that Ian Okell has no argument with the practice, but I feel it is often too diffuse and insufficiently focussed to be of any practical use.

This is a subject with a great deal of biblical grounding, and a positive library of books offering finely nuanced explanations of how different commentators think prayer does, or doesn't work. I've even read some of them. But I don't think the answer to my problem with this area lies in Jesuitical hair splitting, it's much more personal and instinctive than that.

I find that being asked to pray for groups of people such as, *'All those less fortunate than ourselves'*, or *'The victims of the recent flooding in Bangladesh*,' is meaningless and impossible to comply with. It's the sort of request likely to bring the whole notion of prayer into disrepute.

Sympathy with such people and a desire to be helpful in some way, is a basic attribute of humanity, but prayer does not seem to me to be the right approach. Giving money to build a well, or paying to establish a school might be helpful, but mouthing polite words in church and calling it prayer is not. To regard prayer as no more than a synonym for hope is a serious error, I do not believe them to be the same thing, it is linguistically lazy and spiritually pointless.

Médecins sans Frontières, or the US Navy might help the survivors of an earthquake in Haiti, but I am unconvinced that my prayers on the subject will. Such prayers seem to be no more than an expression of benevolence, or general good will.

The man who claims to love all men equally, actually loves nobody but himself. We're back to the Pharisee in the Temple, thanking God that he is not as other men, and then going home satisfied that he's done his bit.

I think that prayer should be something much more personal and focussed, almost laser like in its intensity. In what is perhaps a selfish admission, I would find it extremely difficult to pray for anyone I hadn't met, or at least, didn't know the name of. Not impossible, just very difficult. I'm aware that severely limits the number of people in this world for whom I might pray, but I would point out that, as with Pyramid Selling Schemes, the numbers involved in such interlinked groups don't need to go through very many steps to reach millions.

An objection to this attitude might be that I'm only prepared to pray in cases where my own actions in everyday life can affect the outcome, thus muddying the waters about the cause of any benefit. I don't just accept that, I agree with it and welcome it. I regard one of the functions of prayer as being to concentrate one's mind on the matter in hand, and if that prompts you to do something else, as well as praying, then so much the better.

If you read the words of The Lord's Prayer - Jesus' own words, you will find them to be very tightly focussed indeed. There is nothing remotely vague about, 'Give us this day our daily bread, and forgive us our trespasses.' That is just about as specific as it's possible for the language to be, and it's about a known individual - you. *All those less fortunate than ourselves* don't even get a mention. This is a prayer about the will of God, about your own behaviour and your own environment, which one can safely assume will then have a knock on affect on those in your immediate proximity, and that's as far as it goes.

Prayer at that level can, and I think often does, make a difference. I have always regarded the strength of such prayer, even if only slight, to be incremental, to be worth doing alone but best as a group - even with individually targeted prayers.

A sense of shared endeavour is one of the more compelling reasons for attending church, particularly one where you're a known member of the community. However, even if the only effect of prayer was the change it made to your own behaviour, I would still think it worth doing.

Having decided that prayer for a few named individuals is a good thing, even a helpful thing, why *not* pray for more people? Why *not* spread the happiness and pray for all people? Because that is what the military call 'mission creep', and that is always bad.

The Americans sent less than two hundred advisors to assist the South Vietnamese resist aggression, and ended up with more than half a million men on the ground and national humiliation. That's mission creep. The European Union was set up to promote the basic principles of trade cooperation between six countries and ended up ruining the economies of southern Europe, encouraging war in the Ukraine and dictating the shape of bananas. More mission creep. The road to hell is paved with good intentions.

Whenever prayer loses its focus and tries to be all things to all men it doesn't just cease to be effective, it becomes positively unhelpful, it makes you think you've done something, when you haven't.

Praying for the survivors of some natural disaster is about making *you* feel good, whereas practical assistance in supplying say, emergency accommodation or whatever, is about making *them* feel good. I am most emphatically not saying you can't, or even shouldn't, do both, but you do need to be aware of this significant difference.

I don't want to get too abstruse or rarefied on this subject but there is something else that might be worth considering. Once you've got past the strange idea, implicit in prayer, that the most successful Christians are the ones who pray the loudest and the longest, the ones who are the most persistent God botherers, there is still a problem.

If the sort of prayer I mentioned earlier, for those less fortunate etc, were to be successful, in other words the prayer would cause something to happen which would not otherwise have happened, then where would that leave free will? If every piece of human behaviour that we don't care for could be prayed away, where would that leave the human ability to choose morality over immorality? The ability to make a conscious and individual choice between those two states, and then try to live by that, has to be seen as one of the more essential differences between human beings and animals.

Considering the sheer amount of nastiness in this world, and considering, as just one of many possible examples, that the Chinese leader Mao Zedong knowingly and deliberately caused the deaths of many tens of millions of his own people, a belief in free will is a last defence against madness and suicide. I think that, horrible though it is, the possibility of suffering, or even its certainty, is the price we all have to pay for self determination.

Effective all encompassing prayer and the operation of free will are incompatible. Human progress, as well as personal salvation, can only come about if people are able to make a free choice about their own behaviour, and then live or die with the results. I'm beginning to sound like a mad scientist here, but I've got the bit between my teeth and I'm going with it.

This is the only possible answer to people who demand to know how there could possibly be a loving God when some great tragedy or crime has occurred. How could a loving God have stood by and watched *this* happen?

If you believe in the most basic Christian dogma of all, that personal salvation is possible as a result of personal faith, then you have no choice but to accept that the requisite freedom of action will sometimes produce the most horrible side of humanity, as well as sometimes, the best. If this seems to be an unsatisfactorily short answer to a very big question, there isn't a lot I can do about that, I still think it's the right answer. Free will is an absolute state, like virginity, you either have it or you don't.

I agree that I might feel differently if I found myself in Auschwitz, or my child had been murdered, but the overriding personal rage that such an event could produce is the best possible reason for not allowing our justice system to be run by the relatives of murder victims.

The red mist of revenge, the desire to lash out when hurt, and whatever havoc that wreaks, is understandable, natural even; don't say you wouldn't feel it if you haven't been there. However it should not become the basis of our moral code, and neither does it invalidate religious belief.

To say that the fear of death is discomforting or that ambition is a close first cousin to greed, is to do no more than state the obvious. But when you think how necessary ambition and the fear of death are to all kinds of progress; scientific, medical and intellectual, it becomes clear just how stagnant and immobile a contented society would be. Another word for contented is of course, complacent.

Wanting the world to be permanently and in every way at peace is the sort of desire that prompts the warning - be careful what you wish for. Jesus said that the poor are always with us, well so are the unpleasant, it's part of the human condition.

Having got that off my chest I'm left with what might be called the factual, or technical problems. Those parts of the New Testament which I said earlier I

136

thought to be unlikely, implausible or downright wrong, where I think the text fails to conform to historical or common sense realities.

CHAPTER ELEVEN

Judas Wept
- the cost of love and loss.

The first of these problem areas for me is the story of Judas, and the great betrayal. On purely logical, rather than religious grounds, I have always thought there was something not quite right about this story. I'll go into that shortly, before I do, however, I would like to address one possibility that has been raised by several writers on this subject. That is the recurring suggestion that Judas was not in fact a real person, but just an embodiment of the eternal Jew, with the very name itself meaning Jew.

There are even suggestions that Judas and Jesus were the same person. That's one of the constant delights about biblical studies, you never need to dig very far to reach the lunatic fringe. I just hope that I don't sound like one of them, although I do recognise that to address this subject at all is to run that risk.

The proposal is usually that the inclusion of this *fictional* figure into the story is just another part of the attempt to lay the blame for Jesus' death solely at the Jewish door, whilst exonerating the Romans. This at a time when seeking converts from within orthodox

Judaism had ceased to be the main focus of the Christ movement, whereas coming to an accommodation with the Roman authorities was a very high priority. In other words, it was in the gospel writer's interests to be nice to the Romans. While that underlying reason is certainly valid, I dismiss the suggested method for straightforward practical reasons.

If he had been invented then it is unlikely he would have been given the same name as another disciple, this requires them both to be described in greater detail than is convenient. The betrayer is described as exactly that, or as 'Iscariot', or as, 'The son of Simon.' The other Judas is referred to as, 'The son of James', or 'Not Iscariot', or by the alternative name of Thaddaeus.

Furthermore, if Judas Iscariot is fictional then who was the other original disciple that he replaced? After the death or disappearance of Judas, despite having many other more pressing concerns, the remaining eleven took immediate steps to replace him, and after listing the qualifications for the position, they short listed two candidates. Being quite unable to choose between two strong contenders, they resorted to drawing lots, but if both candidates were acceptable, then why not have them both? The reason being that a total of thirteen disciples would have been as unacceptable as eleven, there were twelve tribes of Israel and there were always going to be twelve disciples.

This means that if Judas was a fictional insert into a pre existing list of disciples, that list would have already had twelve names on it. If he was a later addition, he must have replaced a genuine, but subsequently concealed disciple. As a cover up, the whole process has now grown to be too involved, unwieldy and difficult to manage.

Amendments to the historical account of Jesus' ministry for the purposes of following someone else's agenda, and there are several, tend to be much more direct, almost brutal. The account of Pilate's role at the trial of Jesus isn't hinted at or alluded to; a variety of wildly improbable conciliatory platitudes are brazenly put into Pilate's mouth, to show the Roman Procurator as a refined and sensitive man. The historical fact, however, as we shall see in the next chapter, is that he was an extremely nasty piece of work who was most unlikely to have said any of the things attributed to him.

Similarly, the downplaying of Mary Magdalen's role in Jesus' life isn't handled cautiously, it's more like a bull in a china shop. A comparison of the number of references to her in the canonical gospels, with those in the non canonical gospels reveals a startling disparity. Although she is frequently mentioned, it still looks as if Magdalen references in the canonical gospels have been removed on a wholesale basis; for reasons that I'll come to later.

The comparison of these 'known' amendments in other areas, with the Judas story, and the overall feel of the betrayal narrative, convince me that, whilst the exact details of his role have almost certainly been tampered with, Judas was a real person, and involved in the betrayal of Jesus.

Returning to my original concern, the grit in the oyster; I have always thought there was something that didn't add up in the betrayal story, the closer you look at it, the less readily the different parts fit together. I could never accept that the one disciple who, alone of the twelve, seemed to be a necessary and indispensable part of the story should be dammed to hell for his troubles.

Then I came across a mid eighteenth century essay in the collected works of Thomas De Quincey, otherwise best known for his book, 'Confessions of an English Opium Eater'. His work, which he said was based on earlier German writings, crystallised a lot of my own thoughts and I have relied on that essay to act as the skeleton on which some of my own comments rest. I extend my thanks to him, post mortem, for his help.

To begin at the beginning; although mentioned in all four Gospels, the biographical detail is slim for such a well known figure. A summary of our biblical information is that he was the son of Simon Iscariot and so probably came from Kerioth, a backwater town in southern Judea.

He was one of the twelve disciples and was said to 'hold the common purse', in other words he was their treasurer and handled the cash. It is said that he behaved in a mean and small minded manner over cash at the house of Martha and Mary. Jesus identified him at the Last Supper as the one who would betray him and went on to say that it would be better for him if he had not been born. Judas betrayed the location of Jesus to the High Priests for thirty pieces of silver, and then accompanied the arrest party, identifying Jesus in the dark by kissing him. He then repented and tried to return the money, but the High Priests refused to take it, so he threw it on the ground and went away and hanged himself in remorse.

Each of the events mentioned has other slight peripheral details in the four main Gospels, but that, in essence, is the extent of our biblical sourced information. Apart from these stated facts, the most solidly based inference we can make is that he must have been in some way better educated or qualified than most of the other disciples for him to have been made their treasurer. Anything else we think we know about him is from non canonical sources and folklore. Even of the supposed facts which are scriptural, by far the most significant, his motive, is almost certainly wrong. He wasn't in it for the money.

Could this man, who the Gospels have already painted as unendingly mean and greedy, really have been seized by the overwhelming degree of remorse described in the bible. Would such a man have thrown back the thirty pieces of silver? It looks unlikely to me, I think there's something missing from the story, and I think that with a little digging we can work out what that is.

This can be compared to the divorce of two people, both of whom you know equally well. You listen to the husband's version of events and you think that what he has to say is interesting, perhaps compelling, perhaps entirely true; but at the back of your mind you know there's another version of exactly the same events, equally interesting, compelling and true, but which paints a very different picture. With Judas we have been given just one side of the story, and that's the case for the prosecution.

In order to examine his behaviour we must start with a close look at his beliefs. Judas shared the other disciple's understanding that there was to be an imminent earthly kingdom under the auspices of Jesus. This was the established mainstream position of all the twelve and did not mark Judas out as special. In both Mark and Luke, Jesus is quoted as saying that the kingdom of God would come within the lifetime of people then living. When the crowds welcoming Jesus' triumphal entry into Jerusalem shouted, 'Blessed is the coming kingdom of our ancestor David,' they weren't expecting to wait until they were dead to get there. Even Joseph of Arimathea was said to be waiting expectantly for the kingdom of God.

When asked directly when such a kingdom would come, Jesus' replies were long and complex, containing no specific time frame and, as with many of the parables, the disciples are reported not to have understood their master's teachings. This left the apostles with the unchanged and justifiable belief that the kingdom of God could, and probably would, come to pass at any time.

A significant difference between Judas and the others was that he seems to have speculated more actively on a *reason* for Jesus failing to introduce this kingdom immediately. All available indicators suggested the time was right for early action. The constantly simmering messianic fervour of the Jewish people, mixing and mingling uneasily with a more straightforward political independence movement; the warning messages of the charismatic, almost pop star like figure of John the Baptist, 'Make straight the way of the Lord'; produced a revolutionary ferment throughout Judea. Whatever happened next, the status quo was unlikely to continue.

Even amongst apolitical Jews, if there were any, and the religiously apathetic, there would have been a general resentment of Roman occupation and of their repeated interference in Jewish public and religious affairs.

This was a deeply volatile and unstable situation which could, on the slightest pretext, turn violent and even lead to a full scale attempt to throw off the Roman occupation. Such a revolt, even if supported by the broad mass of the Jewish people and then effectively and efficiently led, would still be of very doubtful outcome, and would in turn lead to brutal repression.

The one missing element in this tinder box of resentment and expectation, and the one thing that might tip the balance from failure to success was the nature of the Jewish leader. A good general might give the Romans a bloody nose, but would that be enough? The Romans had plenty of their own good generals. But a divinely appointed general, a messianic leader of the Jewish people, a new heir to the throne of David; that could change the whole picture. These facts are not just evident in hindsight but were fully understood by both Jews and Romans at the time.

Jesus fulfilled this role exactly, even amongst those not accepting that he was the son of God, all the disciples recognised this and none of them could understand why he hesitated. Jesus' fitness for this role was confirmed, rather than damaged, by the Jewish hierarchy's hostility to him, as that hierarchy was widely seen to be a Roman puppet authority.

Can we be sure the disciples were wrong to think that Jesus himself had considered this? The prize on offer was the possibility of an earthly kingdom, the restoration of the throne of Solomon and David, an anointed Messiah; the security of Jerusalem and a temple pure and undefiled by pagans. It was everything that a devout Jew had ever prayed for.

The story of Satan tempting Jesus on the mountain top, by showing him all the kingdoms of the earth, and saying – 'All the power and the glory can be yours', confirms the existence of this train of thought; the possibility that Jesus would institute or take over an earthly kingdom. Though Jesus' reply, 'Get thee behind me Satan', makes clear his rejection.

But the political and religious hot house of first century Palestine was hardly the place to encourage cool and rational thought, and difficult though it is to admit the fact, Jesus' own ambiguous replies to direct questions over the time scale, did nothing to calm matters.

I think it worth repeating that all Jesus' closest companions, including Judas, believed in the imminent arrival of the kingdom of God on earth, and more of Jesus' recorded sayings support that view than any other. And remember, that as far as Jesus being the son of God is concerned, how much difference is there in the common mind between being a leader who was the son of God, and a divinely appointed king who was sent by God?

How did the apostles view Jesus in this context? They knew him to be a gifted preacher, healer and teacher - their exact views on his divinity *at that time*, seem to have been rather confused and unformed. Their absolute certainty about Jesus' divinity seems only to have come about after his death. But was Jesus temperamentally suited, or even interested in, the mundane routine of running an earthly kingdom?

There are repeated injunctions to 'Leave your family and follow me,' and yet the family was the building block of the tribe and the tribe was the building block of the state. Then in Matthew: 'Do not store up for yourselves treasures on earth, where moth and rust consume,' and again, 'Do not worry about tomorrow, for tomorrow will bring worries of its own.' These are disturbing and uncertain pointers about the farsightedness and preparedness of a proposed earthly leader.

Judas and the others must have been aware of this dichotomy: so many signs that the time was right for the earthly kingdom of God and yet God's chosen messenger on earth was either unwilling or unsuited to the practicalities of action to achieve this.

The Jewish people were seriously weakened by factionalism. Monty Python's film 'The Life of Brian' might have made fun of the murderous rivalries between the Judean People's Front and the People's Front of Judea, but the reality of first century Palestine was probably even more divided.

A national leader of Jesus' stature and authority was the only hope of overcoming this; at that point the popular feeling was that once united the Jewish people could and would sweep the Romans aside. The only problem, it seemed to Judas, was how to precipitate Jesus onto such a course, which, once started, could well be unstoppable.

In the long term the full weight of Imperial Roman power was unbeatable by any Jewish army, no matter how united or well led. However, if the Legions could ever be swept conclusively, even if only temporarily, from Palestine, that might have inclined such a very practical people as the Romans, to come to some accommodation with the local ruler. It had happened under the militarily and diplomatically successful Herod the Great, whom the Romans had installed as the semi autonomous ruler of all Judea, able to govern internally as he saw fit, and only constrained to follow the Roman line in external affairs. That arrangement came about despite the fact that Herod was not even a full blood Jew and cordially detested by most of the population.

In contrast, Jesus, who was genuinely and widely popular and in the lineage of the House of David, would have been the natural recipient of such an arrangement. And that situation would, for most of his disciples and followers, have been seen as the full vindication of his ministry.

The rule of King Jesus of Judea was exactly what so many of them were working towards, that would have been the long awaited Kingdom of God mentioned so often by the prophets and by Jesus himself. The fact that Jesus had a completely different sort of kingdom in mind was not widely, if at all, understood.

Another significant difference between Judas and the other disciples was that whilst none of them fully understood Jesus' message, Judas alone seems to think that he did. He believed that if Jesus were arrested by the temple authorities he would have no option but to use his divinity either to escape, thus showing the world his power, or to summon earthly support, thus precipitating the Jewish uprising with Jesus at its head.

The possibility of Jesus meekly accepting arrest, condemnation and execution had clearly never occurred to him. He was ready to act, surely the others would be too.

It is probable that, as an educated man and the disciple's treasurer, he was sufficiently worldly wise and politically aware to be confident that his calculations in this matter were more likely to be correct than those of his more rustic brothers. To say that this was over confidence is more apparent in retrospect, at the time it would have seemed a realistic assessment. Yet without Jesus' cooperation in taking the next step, none of this could happen.

Jesus was undoubtedly the disciples' teacher and master, but the relationship between them was never a one way street. Suggestions flowed in both directions; as is shown in John 7 when his companions told him to leave Galilee and go to Judea for greater public exposure and to win more converts.

Even the Lord's Prayer was only given to the disciples after a specific request for such a prayer. Judas's belief that Jesus might need to be prompted into action was not some new and startling departure from previous behaviour. In the circumstances, it is difficult not to accept that his desire to force Jesus' hand, to prompt his friend and teacher into action, was more a display of love and loyalty, than treachery.

As the events following Jesus' arrest unfolded, implacably and terrifyingly, it will have rapidly become clear that far from helping to introduce the kingdom of God, he had in fact betrayed his master.

His intended help had become a poisoned cup, and worse, he is not reported to have discussed his reasoning with the other disciples; they would have only seen his actions. After such an outcome there would have been few volunteers to say, 'Yes, that seemed like a good idea to me as well'. Following the crucifixion, Judas was untouchable, no one would even admit to understanding his motives, let alone agreeing with them. The isolation must have intensified his guilt.

Judas's reported disappearance or death occurred at a time when the very existence of the disciples as a coherent group engaged in the same venture, underwent its most severe test. A natural fear of arrest, torture and execution by either the Temple authorities or the Romans must certainly have been a prime factor in driving them underground.

It's a very strange and unnatural human being, no matter how divinely inspired, who doesn't fear the prolonged agony of crucifixion. The High Priests, with Roman assistance, had dealt with the movement's ringleader and it must have seemed entirely probable that they would then move on to deal with his principal lieutenants. This was a time for keeping your head down.

Despite his central role in the early church, and Jesus' reference to him as, 'The rock on which I will build my church', I find it very difficult to warm to Peter. His apparent acquiescence with James the Just's assumption of the leadership of the early church in Jerusalem, despite James being a pedantic and uninspiring man, with no visible qualifications for the role, looks, from this perspective, to be inexplicable or simply weak. Worse still, his later quarrels with Paul, over the necessity for circumcision and Jewish dietary laws, make him look vacillating and contradictory.

I acknowledge unreservedly Peter's subsequent bravery and tireless evangelism but, in neither of the areas mentioned above, could I imagine myself to have been on his side. It might be impertinent for me to judge the actions of a saint by my own low standards, but as they are the only standards I have, they are all I can offer.

However, the one aspect of his behaviour that is routinely criticised, his three times denial of any connection with Jesus on the night of his arrest, looks to me more like rational prudence than cowardice. It might not have felt very noble at the time, but for the essential good of the cause, a motto of Live to Fight Another Day, when viewed in isolation, is difficult to condemn.

The trouble is that when you take that action together with what happened at the crucifixion then a more worrying picture emerges. A simple list of the names of Jesus' friends at the foot of the cross tells a fascinating story all on its own. Mary Magdalen, mentioned most frequently; Mary the mother of Jesus; her sister Mary Cleopas, the mother of James the Just and Mary the mother of the disciples John and James. (This biblical repetition of certain names can be confusing, I've laid it out as clearly as I can, but sometimes you just need to puzzle your way through.)

John's Gospel also mentions that 'The Disciple who Jesus loved' was present, standing next to Jesus' mother. The identity of this disciple is unknown and I will briefly discuss the possible candidates in a later chapter, suffice it to say that however you look at it, it isn't likely to be Peter.

Four women called Mary and one possible, unidentified, fifth person. Not a single named one of the twelve male disciples is mentioned, and it is inconceivable they could have been there without being named. One might suggest that the women were not under the same pressure to evade the authorities as the twelve, but that doesn't bear scrutiny. All those women are stated to have followed Jesus in his ministry and to have provided for him, so they would have been as well known to the authorities as any of the twelve.

After the disorganised melee of Jesus' night time arrest in the Garden of Gethsemane the disciples were forced to flee for their lives, and in fairness Jesus had specifically forbidden them from trying to prevent the arrest. But how long did it take them to gather their wits and reassemble?

It would seem that at least some of them gathered during the following two days at the house of John Mark's mother, inevitably another Mary, but wherever they were, they were there in secret. This is not to deny the dangers they were avoiding were real, perhaps the women's action in attending the crucifixion was foolhardy, but that isn't the point. The point here is not what you or I think of the participant's actions, that's interesting but unimportant; what matters is what the remaining eleven disciples thought of their own behaviour.

I cannot believe that they, especially Peter, were not ashamed of their ready abandonment of Jesus, of their failure to offer support to him as he died. This is particularly so when compared to the women's actions. And it is that very point which makes their treatment of Judas a foregone conclusion, they were ashamed of their own inaction and needed someone else to point a finger at - someone else's behaviour to divert attention away from their own.

If Judas was expecting anyone to stand up and say they understood or sympathised with his attempt to help Jesus fulfil biblical prophecy, to acknowledge that whatever the outcome, his motives were pure, then he was doomed to disappointment. In fact he was doomed, full stop. Judas, the traitor, was too convenient to all parties for there to be any hope of a different verdict. Immediate convenience is the mainspring to a great deal of human behaviour.

Returning to a slightly wider view; the abiding problem in this story must be; how could the son of God, a person possessed of divine knowledge, not know that Judas, a man he mixed with daily, would betray him?

The astonishingly simple answer is, of course, that he did know. According to the Gospels he not only knew that he would be betrayed, he knew by whom, and for the avoidance of doubt said so clearly and repeatedly.

But answering that question simply raises a much larger one: if Jesus knew he was to be betrayed then why did he allow the betrayal to proceed, it would have been the work of a moment to tell the others and stop Judas's plan in its tracks. Furthermore, in strict moral terms, the knowledge that another person is about to sin, and to have it within your power to prevent that, but fail to do so, is in itself a sin. In legal terms this would be termed as being an accessory before the fact.

That might sound like a foolish quibble over a small detail, but it isn't. To have watched Judas plan to sin, prepare to sin and then to commit that sin, and yet to choose not to intervene can only mean that the fact of Judas's actions were considered more important than the sin itself. That is an aspect of the story which receives no mention in the Gospel versions of the great betrayal.

The report of Judas's death in Matthew states that he hanged himself, whereas in Acts it is stated that he, 'Fell headlong and his bowels gushed out,' a rather unlikely result of hanging oneself. More likely, such a term is no more to be taken literally than saying a rejected lover has had their heart broken. Even more probable is that these reports of his death are simply the easiest way to remove him permanently from the story. The derogatory references to his character; he was a thief, he was a mean spirited penny pincher at Martha and Mary's house, are no more than post mortem smears to further blacken the name of a man you wish to be rid of.

That the other disciples were horrified by the presence of an apparent traitor in their midst seems obvious, and their desire to see him gone, without troubling to ask the question *Why*, is understandable. His was immediately portrayed as the greatest betrayal known to man, he had betrayed the son of God.

But the story of Judas can never be about Judas alone, it is about the relationship between Jesus himself and the circle of his closest followers. The speed and completeness of the disciples' rejection of Judas was

153

caused by more than just his convenience as a scapegoat, someone to cover the shame of their own perceived cowardice.

The more perceptive of Jesus' followers must have entertained at least the suspicion that any one of them might have done the same. It might not have been openly discussed, in fact I would guess that it wasn't, but some of them must have asked themselves if they too might not have decided to 'help' Jesus. They all held the same view of Christ's mission on earth, it was simply that Judas felt it more deeply and then did something about it, something that he sincerely believed would be helpful; something that would reveal Christ in his glory.

Please don't throw things at me for saying this, but there are solid grounds for seeing Judas as the first Christian martyr.

Once that basic situation is understood, then a previously puzzling and badly plotted story begins to make sense. Judas acted with the full knowledge and acquiescence of Jesus. Their motives might have differed, Judas wanted to prompt his master into earthly action, whereas Jesus wanted to fulfil the words of the prophet and shed his own blood for the sins of humanity. But condemnation of Judas's motives has never been what made him the most reviled man in history, he occupies that position because of his actions, and yet those actions were necessary for the fulfilment of Jesus', and thus God's plan.

Assuming that Judas Iscariot was a genuine historical figure, which I do, and not just a narrative pivot around which the plot could swing, then we need to treat him as a human being in his own right, with his own motives and responsibilities. In doing that, and having considered everything else, we seem to be left

154

with two questions; how sinful can a man be who acts from love, to fulfil God's purpose? And, would you cheerfully condemn that man to hell for doing so - albeit with his mixed motives?

There is just one final note before leaving Judas, if you're tempted to learn more by reading the Gospel of Judas, a mid second century gnostic text, about which the only certainty is that it was not written by Judas, then you may be disappointed. It contains no new insights that I could find, beyond reporting that Jesus laughed at his disciples, and unless you're a trained academic in that area, it needs to be read with the aid of explanatory footnotes. Thomas De Quincey's take on the subject, mentioned at the beginning of this section, is a far more rewarding read.

CHAPTER TWELVE

Pontius Pilate
- what are the chances?

My next area of concern in the New Testament is the account of Jesus' trial before Pilate, a story I have always found to be filled with improbabilities. Some New Testament characters, such as Peter or Paul, may be largely judged by their actions, with their motives either obvious, or inferred therefrom. However, the actions of Judas and Pilate can only be understood when seen in the full light of their motives or backgrounds.

I suppose it may be said that everyone's actions spring from their motives, after all I only wrote this book in the confident expectation of vast wealth and international acclaim, which makes me fairly transparent. Though there is still that reminder on my desk to put in more sex and violence, which might change your mind.

The difference arises when a person's motives are not apparent and yet those motives markedly change the outcome, which is the case with Judas. In Pilate's case, when his background and track record in other areas are taken into account, they make the New Testament story completely untenable. For that reason I want to look at whatever we can see of Pilate from other sources, in the hope that what we find may shine a clearer light on the man.

Nothing is known for certain of his origins, there are several apocryphal tales, mostly medieval, variously suggesting that he was born at any one of a number of sites across Italy, Spain, Germany or Scotland. Such a range of possible origins might sound unlikely, but is in fact quite possible.

While it was not routine for even senior administrative or military officers to take their families with them on overseas postings, it did happen. Evidence of that is plain from the fact that Augustus issued a decree forbidding it, a decree which subsequently had to be rescinded. It is also worth remembering that the legions routinely recruited both officers and men from the constituent states of the Empire, which then included most of Europe, the Middle East and North Africa.

The Roman legions were not filled with Romans, they were filled with colonials, and the progression from senior military rank to civilian rank was well established. Thus it was not uncommon for even a Senator or an Emperor to have been born overseas. More than 2000 years before the Americans decided to be the world's melting pot, the Roman Empire was already doing it.

The version of his origins that I prefer, has Pilate coming from Spanish nobility, joining the legions as a staff officer and then moving to Rome. Despite Spaniards at that time having a reputation in Rome as little better than gigolos, pimps and con men, he somehow managed to secure the hand of Claudia Procula, a historically uncertain figure, said to have been the granddaughter of the previous Emperor, Augustus.

One of the reasons for preferring this version of his origins is that it was accepted as fact in the earliest years of the church that Pilate's wife had imperial blood, and this is the only account containing that detail. It is from the apocryphal gospels, mostly second century, that we have her name, and this is a much earlier date than any of the alternatives.

Wherever he came *from,* we can definitively place him in Judea in 26 AD, when he arrived from Rome to take up the governorship of that province. Early Christian writers disagree about his wife's beliefs, sayings and actions, and even the spelling of her name but they all agree that she was with him in Judea, and most that she was of the Imperial line. His formal rank was an 'eques', or Roman knight, and as such he was technically the Prefect of Judea; but it feels more natural for this account to use his more common title of governor.

The minimum age for such an appointment was thirty, and whilst we don't know his actual age we can take a reasonable guess. Working from the fact that there is no known record of any prior service in Rome, together with the immaturity of some of his actions in Judea, suggest that he was probably still in his early thirties. In other words, he was more or less of an age with Jesus.

No likeness of his physical appearance survives, but the fashion at that time would have been for a man of his age and rank to have had short hair and been clean shaven. A picture is beginning to emerge of someone we can almost recognise from today. This short haired, clean shaven young man, who must have been on the make and eager to advance himself, or he wouldn't have got either the girl or the appointment. A young man from a slightly questionable background who was probably sensitive on the issue, but had still managed to marry well above his station, and then parley that achievement into getting himself a governorship.

The modern diplomatic service would have probably been too tightly regulated for his taste, but he would surely have slotted easily into some modern international business, perhaps banking would have been sufficiently corrupt and ruthless. We see him, newly arrived at his first major posting, with his upmarket trophy wife by his side and the judicial power of life and death over the local population.

The governor's duties were primarily; military security, maintaining a level of domestic stability necessary for the collection of taxes, and ensuring the continuance of cross border trade, mainly with Rome. This was what was usually known as the Pax Romana, the Roman view of what constituted a stable and secure way of life. What he was not interested in was the local administration of justice or local politics, where these things did not affect Rome's international interests.

Any Roman governor's degree of interference with the local religion was deliberately slight, the Empire was well aware how sensitive such an issue could be and took a very relaxed and tolerant attitude to their subjects beliefs. Governors and military officers were under orders not to interfere, unless such practices threatened civil order or political stability. Give Caesar his due and after that you can worship who or what you want: a golden image, a man, a sacred mountain or a big woolly dog - we don't care.

The possible difficulty with that approach, especially in Judea, was the fact that Caesar was at that time himself regarded as a God, and decisions had to be taken as to which God took priority. Did local religious symbols and duties take priority over Imperial Roman symbols and duties? Jesus' famous answer to this problem was; 'Render unto Caesar that which is Caesar's, and unto God that which is God's.'

The reality of daily life throughout the Empire was that the parties involved usually managed to come to some practical accommodation with each other, it was in everybody's interests to do so. The Latin phrase *modus vivendi* says it all, a working arrangement. It only became a problem when one side of the equation was too dogmatic or bull headed to accept the requirement for daily power sharing. Yes, you have to acknowledge the rights of the all conquering Empire, but no, you don't pointlessly aggravate the natives.

This was precisely the balancing act that a provincial governor was required to undertake on a daily basis, it wasn't some special requirement over and above his other duties, it was at the very heart of what he was being paid for. A fair test of any governor's skill is how well he fulfilled that requirement.

Much of what follows is taken from two principal sources, first the writings of the commentator and historian Josephus. Born in Jerusalem in 37 AD of high class Jewish parents, he went on to be a revolutionary leader of the Galilean forces in the first Jewish Roman war which started in 66 AD. Following a military defeat, he surrendered to the Roman general Vespasian. Thereafter, for reasons that are too involved to be worth pursuing here, he became Romanised, eventually becoming a Roman citizen and an Imperial advisor. Opinion is still divided as to exactly how much of a traitor he was, if at all. What is clear is that he is an unrivalled source of information about the New

Testament era in Palestine; much or our detailed knowledge of political and religious events in that region, and the personalities involved, come from him. He shows some slight occasional bias, but overall seems to be trustworthy.

The second main source is a man called Philo, a well educated exact contemporary of Pilate's, who was the son in law of the previous High Priest, Annas. He was well connected with both the occupation forces and with the Jewish ruling class. He was one of the elite Jews who saw the Romans as a useful tool to help maintain the status quo and defend the privileges of the ruling class. He was the sort of Jew who was more at home with high class Romans than with low class Jews; in the Second World War he would have been called a collaborator.

His connections might make him sound like a useful source, but owing to his attempts to promote a competing candidate for the governorship, he has a noticeable bias, particularly against Pilate. So while it is interesting to read him referring to Pilate's stubbornness, cruelty, venality, violence, savage ferocity, frequent executions without trial and so on, it is useful to remember that while all these things might very well be true, it is also a fact that Philo could be following his own agenda.

The Roman province of Judea, incorporated Idumea and Samaria, and stretched from the edge of Galilee in the north, to the southern end of the Dead Sea, about eighty miles north to south with Jerusalem at its heart. It was not a top ranking posting for a Roman governor, neighbouring Egypt and Syria were both far more important, and this was shown in the size of the military garrison that was allocated.

Pilate had between 3000 and 4000 military auxiliaries under his direct command, second rate troops with Roman officers. Owing to a dispensation granted by Augustus, no recruitment was permitted in the pre Roman territory of Judea itself, nonetheless most were still local, from neighbouring places such as Samaria and Galilee. This sometimes showed itself by their taunting and acts of provocation to their fellow countrymen, Frequently behaving in a way that properly disciplined professional troops never would. It was a constant low level irritant to the population, and while not likely to cause a revolt in itself, it provided an uncomfortable background to other events.

If the security situation turned ugly then Pilate could call for help from the governor of Syria, formally referred to as the Roman legate, and Pilate's immediate superior, who had four full strength legions at his disposal. For a while, units of the Tenth Fretensis Legion were, at Pilate's request, temporarily seconded from Syria to Judea, but it was never a permanent arrangement.

One of the reasons why Judea had not been ranked as posing the highest level of military risk was the existence of such potential adversaries as the German tribes, the Gauls and the Parthians on the Syrian border. They were the ones to watch, the big beasts prowling watchfully around the edges of Empire, always ready to sink their teeth into any local weakness.

Compared to them, Judea seemed like a watched pot that wasn't going to boil over anytime soon. Everybody knew about the Jews, they complained a lot, they went on endlessly about their God and they moaned about the occupation; but then they always had and probably always would. What they needed was a level headed man in the governor's palace, a man who could sweet talk the locals, maintain the status quo and avoid kicking over anything breakable; someone to keep the lid on things while the important stuff went on elsewhere.

What they got was the untried Pilate, keen to make a name for himself. On its own, that wasn't enough to cause a disaster, most disasters are the result of a chain of events but, as we shall see, he managed to make himself a link in that chain for reasons that aren't even hinted at in the bible.

The precise areas of responsibility in the administration of justice, between the Jewish Councils, known as the greater and lesser Sanhedrins and the Roman authorities, can be made as complex as you like. There are the standard Imperial guidelines, there are areas of local custom and usage, there are religious sensibilities and then of course the ever present: exceptional circumstances. To avoid turning this into a legal textbook, it is easier to say that the governor judged all cases likely to result in a death penalty, and the local authorities handled the rest.

The standard Roman method of execution was crucifixion, this wasn't something unusual, pulled like a rabbit from a hat, especially for Jesus; it was in everyday use all over the Empire. It was a hideous and lingering death, sometimes up to three days, and deliberately so, an Imperial statement - if you raise your hand against us - then this is what you get. By the time Pilate sentenced Jesus, he would have already sentenced countless other people to the same death. It was an entirely routine process and, beyond its appalling barbarity, there was nothing extraordinary about it.

The point cannot be made too strongly that the trial of Jesus before Pilate was, and is, only significant to

Christians. Most people have only ever heard Pilate's name in that context, and consequently the importance of that single event in his governorship of Judea has assumed a hugely exaggerated status. This is thoroughly misleading and is one of the reasons why the biblical account of that trial is so rarely challenged - if we rely solely on that version, we have no background against which to set his alleged actions.

The reality is that Pontius Pilate's historical significance, distinctly slim at best, relates to the fact that he was one of many contributory factors to the Jewish revolt which began in 66 AD.

The trial of Jesus; from either Pilate's perspective, or the perspective of the Roman Empire, was a very brief and unimportant event, which those involved with would have considered scarcely worth mentioning. If Pilate's conduct in office is to be considered at all, and I intend to do so, then it should be viewed as a continuous whole, and not just as one isolated, out of context, incident.

As for the Jews, they not only had their own God, like so many other subject peoples, but they believed themselves to be that God's chosen people. That alone was not sufficient to set them apart, what made them unique was the sheer intensity of their belief. Even if such a belief had ever held equal force in other societies under Roman rule, it would not have had the same effect as it did with the Jews. The difference being that only the Jews were a sufficiently coherent society to retain their national and religious identity in exile.

A group of exiled Syrians or Gauls in, for example Rome, were no more than a disparate bunch of foreigners, each of them making their own way as best they could. Whereas a group of exiled Jews in Rome would immediately set up their own synagogue and appoint their own Rabbi, they retained their core identity even in exile. Hence the cry of the wandering Jew: Next Year in Jerusalem.

What all of this meant to the Roman occupying power was simple. If they hit the Jews hard enough to hurt them in Judea, any repercussions would be felt not just in Judea, but throughout the Jewish Diaspora, and that meant throughout the Roman Empire.

This might not have frightened the Romans, they were too powerful and confident for that, but it certainly made them aware of the fact that their behaviour in Judea could have far reaching consequences. All the more reason, you might think, for them to have a pragmatic and accommodating governor, a man who could be relied on to avoid unnecessary provocation. We're back to that same phrase, a *modus vivendi*, live and let live.

It was the established custom for all Roman governors to profit from their time in office. Everyone knew that extortion and bribe taking was illegal, and yet everyone also knew that it went on, exceptions were regarded with astonishment. It was so common that the money handed over to obtain a building permit, or to settle a dispute in your favour, even had its own name. It was called 'ointment', something you rubbed on to make things get better.

This practice only ever attracted official notice and punishment if it became so gross and extortionate as to cause public uproar, or if a governor was under attack for other reasons and additional charges were needed to bulk out the indictment. Yet again, the picture we see is of great latitude being given to a governor; just as long as he kept the taxes flowing, the trade moving and the natives quiet. It was a well understood and perfectly

166

effective system, with a certain level of corruption accepted by all parties.

It's no good saying that by our standards Pilate deserved ten years in jail, he wasn't living in our times, or by our standards. It is exactly that disjuncture, that difference of expectation and action, between his time and our own, that applies right the way through this story. We have to try and view his behaviour by the standards of his day, and not by what we would like to think of as our own.

I phrased that last sentence somewhat uncertainly, because the possibility has just occurred to me that in actual fact our standards might not have changed as much as we could wish. I'm not sure that being a ship's chandler is a particularly corrupt business, but after more than thirty years of being one, with my customers coming from every corner of the globe, I cannot honestly say that I've never paid a bribe; because I have – lots of them.

The payments were often referred to as commissions, but that did nothing to disguise what was going on. My company would be given an order on the understanding that we would remit a cash percentage of the invoice total to the person placing the order. As none of our customers was British and all the payments went through our books as exactly what they were, the practice was at that time perfectly legal, and confirmed as such by counsel's opinion. But was it moral?

My own view is made clear by the fact that it didn't occur to me to list this behaviour in the chapter on my moral failings and shortcomings, it was, and is, the way of the world. Any ship's chandler engaged in international trade who tells you that he doesn't do this is a big fat liar.

167

How do you imagine that fighter jets get sold to Saudi Arabia, or Qatar gets awarded the football World Cup? And it's not just Arabs, it's no different with Russians, Koreans, Chinese or Indians, and a whole lot more. So perhaps we shouldn't be looking at Pilate as a man with first century standards, when it comes to back handers, it's beginning to look as though he's right up to date.

I acknowledge that in what follows some of the conclusions are speculative, but I think the opinions I offer are the most obvious and probable conclusions. To examine anyone's actions after a gap of two thousand years, requires some level of speculation in the search for possible clues to his mindset and personal feelings, which would otherwise have to remain beyond our reach.

The governor's palace was in the luxurious port city of Caesarea, a city built by Herod around thirty years earlier. Most buildings were constructed of white marble and the impression it gave was almost of a miniature version of Rome. There were temples to Roman Gods, baths, an amphitheatre and the lowest percentage of Jewish inhabitants anywhere in Judea. The coastal climate was fresher and cooler in the hot months than the oppressive temperature in Jerusalem, so it's no surprise that Pilate spent the great majority of his time there, it was his seat of government. However, he was obliged to visit Jerusalem for major religious festivals, to show the face of the Roman administration, and to be on hand in the event of civil disorder.

On such visits he occupied what had been Herod's royal palace, another luxurious piece of architecture, designed to make a statement about the magnificence of its builder. All surviving reports speak of how impressive it was, but the one thing that visitors always remarked upon was its size, it was huge.

A palace of that size was well suited to a royal household, which in Herod's case involved a widespread family with multiple spouses, children, relatives and hangers on, together with an army of court officials, servants and slaves. It was Herod's palace, built by him and filled by him, and from it he ruled as king over a country several times larger than the province of Judea. As a slight side issue, Herod's willingness to murder his own family members caused one Roman to remark that you would live a longer life as the half Jewish King's pig than his son.

I picture life at Herod's court as being the sort of existence portrayed in the paintings of the Victorian artist Lawrence Alma-Tadema. A decadent mixture of pleasure seeking luxury and rose petals, with the Roman Empire as its setting and glimpses of the Mediterranean as its backdrop, but with the added risk of sudden death thrown in.

But now, in contrast to such over staffed and flaunting opulence, we have Pontius Pilate. The young upstart governor of a second rate and pared down province who, despite his trophy wife, would have had no more than a handful of personal staff and very few slaves. (One sympathises instinctively, the slave shortage in south Cheshire is a continuing scandal.)

The empty corridors and reception rooms, which he almost certainly couldn't afford to furnish, must have been a daily reminder of his perceived lack of status. Is it possible that he felt the locals were sneering at him for trying, so unsuccessfully, to fill a bigger man's shoes? The comparison must have been unavoidable. As I say, all this is speculative but not remotely improbable, at all events such a situation could be enough to make an insecure man even more determined to assert himself.

On which subject it is time to consider his actions; for the twenty years before his arrival Judea had been peaceful; not somnolent - this wasn't Sleepy Hollow, but in first century Middle Eastern terms, relatively peaceful. With Pilate's arrival all that changed.

One of the best known and central tenets of Judaism is the unacceptability of graven images, and an avoidance of this by the occupying forces was essential to the smooth running of the civil administration. Yet within months of arriving in Judea, Pilate planned to break that understanding. This prohibition was so well known that immature bravado looks more probable than ignorance - he was going to show the Jews just who ran this place.

The Roman legionary standard, the ceremonial decorated pole which every legion carries into battle and guards with its life, had a variety of emblems on it, depending on the legion it represented. One of these was commonly a decorative golden plaque bearing an image of the Emperor. Pilate arranged for a display of these standards to be erected overnight on the walls of the Antonia fortress in the heart of Jerusalem.

This meant that when the citizens emerged the next morning, they were faced with a display of prohibited images, right next door to their Temple. The outrage at this deliberate insult was immediate and widespread.

Pilate was in his usual accommodation at Caesarea, presumably thinking himself far enough away to ignore the protests. Yet within 24 hours a huge crowd had walked the 60 miles from Jerusalem, and this was in midwinter, to gather outside his palace; demanding that the standards be removed.

The crowd is reported to have been quiet, almost polite, but insistent. Pilate refused to agree and tried to ignore them. For several days the standoff continued, the crowd politely demanding, and Pilate flatly refusing. Then on the sixth day he called in the military, who confronted the crowd with drawn swords. The crowd's response was to stand firm and defy the soldiers to do their worst.

This presented Pilate with an almost impossible dilemma. To cause bloodshed on a scale that was sure to come to Rome's attention, for a reason that the Emperor would consider to have been an unnecessary provocation in the first place, would result in his immediate dismissal, or worse. The unpalatable alternative was to bow to Jewish demands and remove the standards, to give in to mob pressure. After some hours of deliberation, he took the only possible decision and ordered the standards be removed. It was a public humiliation.

It was shortly after this that Pilate ordered a change in the local coinage. The Emperor's head appeared on Roman coins throughout the Empire, and these coins were in circulation in Judea, even Jesus handled one. But for the reasons mentioned above that likeness was omitted from specifically Judean coins. Pilate approached this next affront to the Jews more obliquely. Instead of showing the Emperor on the new coins, he showed instead items used in Roman religious services, such as ritual oil vessels and wands. This was undeniably offensive but not quite as much so as the standards had been, and the resultant objections more easily dismissed.

At first sight, the next example of Jewish protests about Pilate's behaviour might be thought of as unjustified, but when you get to the details he's still same man playing the same game. He decided to improve Jerusalem's water supply by building a large new aqueduct, this should surely meet with popular approval. In the list of things that the Romans did to improve civilisation wherever they went, are certain obvious things that are always mentioned; straight roads, a unified legal system and the supply of clean drinking water.

Jerusalem was perennially short of water, this was exactly the sort of scheme a governor should be involved in. If public voting had been invented, this would have been a vote winner. His new aqueduct went from somewhere near Bethlehem, the precise spot is uncertain, to the reservoirs known as Solomon's Pools, from there the water was carried north to Jerusalem through two existing aqueducts.

The first problem could very well have been accidental, the route of the new water supply passed through a cemetery, which it was said rendered the supply ritually unclean. This was perhaps a fact that had been overlooked by the engineers, but could now be fixed in some way. Unfortunately the focus of complaint rapidly settled onto something much more substantial. It turned out that Pilate had not used Roman money for the construction but had somehow got his hands onto the Temple treasury money.

This money was called *corban* and was mainly raised from a tax on all Jewish adults, it was reserved especially for sacred purposes. No matter how beneficial the aqueduct might have been - it wasn't sacred.

The most famous example of the use of *corban* was the payment of 30 pieces of silver to Judas, which he then tried to return to the High Priest, but once it had been in profane hands the cash could not be returned to the treasury. What is not clear at this remove of time is exactly how Pilate managed to get hold of this money, was it a physical raid on the treasury, or was it through the connivance of a corrupt Temple official? However it happened, Josephus assures us that it did, and he has no visible axe to grind on this subject.

Once again there was a public uproar, but this time our man handled it differently, and in a way that shows us something rather nasty about him.

He had been forced to back down over the display of standards, because he'd picked the wrong subject to have an argument on, but they weren't going to catch him the same way twice. He knew there was going to be trouble, and he hadn't the slightest intention of backing down this time, he also knew that Rome would back him over the construction of such a very Roman item as an aqueduct.

He arranged for units of his auxiliary troops to be on hand, but in disguise. All military uniforms and insignia were removed and the men dressed in long flowing robes, as if they were local civilians, beneath which they concealed clubs and swords. Their language, facial features and skin colouring were already local, so the disguise would have been convincing. Jospehus's and Philo's accounts of the ensuing confrontation are graphic and read like part of a film script.

Unlike the quiet protest in Caesarea, this time the crowd were extremely vocal and determined to make their point. Pilate appeared before them, clad in a spotless and gleaming white toga and sat as though ready to give judgement on his X shaped *curule* chair, the official seat of a presiding magistrate.

As the crowd approached he held up his hand and warned them to disperse, they ignored him and continued to approach. Once again he warned them to disperse, again they ignored him. When they were finally within spitting distance, literally within spitting distance, the shaking fists were near enough to make him flinch and the spit was landing on his face and toga, he gave the pre arranged signal. This was a man, certainly not without courage, who revelled in the arrogant thrill of such a close call, particularly when he knew he had an ace up his metaphorical sleeve.

His troops, arranged around the outer edge of the crowd pulled out their clubs and swords and began to lay into everyone within reach. These weren't warning blows with the side of the blade to encourage dispersal, it was wholesale slaughter. Unprepared and unarmed civilians were no match for even second rate troops, especially when those troops were armed and organised and primed to kill.

Apologists have suggested that the death toll was higher than Pilate had anticipated, and was to some extent caused by panic stricken civilians trampling on each other as they tried to flee. But whatever the numbers, or the exact manner of their deaths; Pilate planned it, Pilate ordered it and Pilate sat and watched it happen, making no attempt to halt the slaughter.

In the next of his serial attempts to outrage local opinion, he tried once again to display Imperial emblems, painted shields this time, dedicated to the Emperor, on the walls of Herod's palace in Jerusalem. The story has by now grown too familiar to justify further repetition. Suffice it to say that he displayed them, a letter of complaint was sent to Rome, and Tiberius, the Emperor, instructed him to remove them. There is a sense of obstinate refusal built into the man's character, a complete unwillingness to learn an obvious and repeated lesson.

The point about all this is not that Pilate hates the Jews, that isn't what we're looking at. There is no personal hatred involved, though he certainly dislikes them, he regards them as lesser beings than Romans, and their religion as ridiculous.

The point is that whilst he might be a jumped up Roman parvenu with a poor provincial pedigree - he is still a Roman, and they are not. They are a defeated subject people and he sees it as his job to remind them of that fact, on a daily basis. Had he been the Roman governor of Britain he would have treated Britons in exactly the same way.

The Imperial notion of allowing docile local populations significant autonomy, under a benevolent Roman oversight, is not one that appeals to him. His behaviour is more hard line and aggressive than anything in his instructions authorises. He treads a fine line between annoying the Jews more than he annoys his employer, and for a vindictive and small minded man with poor judgement, that's a dangerous place to be.

On the other side of the divide we have Jesus, the star player who's still waiting to make his first appearance in the story. The reason why he hasn't been mentioned is because despite the proximity in time and geography between our two lead players, there has been no contact between them, even at second or third hand.

All through his ministry Jesus gives no sign of being troubled by the Roman occupation, it's not that he approves of it, he doesn't, but it isn't the Romans who are causing him problems. The people who bother him are all Jewish.

Whenever people are sent to try and trap Jesus into incriminating himself with trick questions, they are always identified as agents of the High priests or the

175

Pharisees. Similarly when John the Baptist is executed, it isn't by the Romans, it's by Herod Antipas, the Jewish ruler of Galilee and Perea. But then that is no more than you would expect, both Jesus and John the Baptist were preaching almost exclusively to Jews, the situation of the two sides ignoring each other was mutual. The story of Jesus and the Romans is a very short one, and it's just about to start.

The actual fact of Jesus' trial before Pilate is beyond dispute, as is the outcome and the crucifixion. That isn't at issue, well not by me anyway. What I dispute is the record of Pilate's conduct in that trial, and what I believe to be the political slant applied to the various gospel accounts of the event.

The first of the gospels to be written was, by common consent, Mark's, between 66 -70 AD. That contains the briefest account of Jesus' trial before Pilate, the central section of which consists of just three quotations. Pilate asks,

'Are you the King of the Jews?'

Jesus replies; 'You say so.'

Then after further charges are laid by the Chief Priest, Pilate asks,

'Have you no answer? See how many charges they bring against you.'

To which Jesus makes no reply. And that, apart from the appeal to the crowd resulting in the release of Barabbas, is the extent of Mark's report.

The next was Matthew's gospel, probably written between the dates 80 - 90 AD. In this Jesus' appearance before Pilate is almost identical to Mark's, except for the addition of the hand washing scene, where Pilate shows that he is not responsible; and his claim after the crowd demand Barabbas's release,

'I am innocent of this man's blood, see to it yourselves.'

To which, it is bizarrely suggested, the crowd shouted, 'His blood be on us and on our children.'

The idea that Pilate should have publically abdicated his role as governor, in favour of mob rule, is beyond belief. This is a man who has repeatedly demonstrated his views on how to deal with a Jewish mob, and that wasn't to agree with their demands.

The third gospel to be written was Luke's, around 80 - 100 AD. In this, as well as the introduction of a new scene where Jesus is temporarily transferred to Herod's custody, the story now contains Pilate's claim,

'I find no basis for an accusation against this man.'

Later he asks, 'What evil has he done? I have found in him no ground for the sentence of death.'

He then repeatedly suggests that Jesus should be simply flogged and released. The story is expanding in the telling, and at every expansion Pilate's guilt is diminishing, and that of the Jews increasing.

Finally there is John's gospel, reckoned to have been written the last, possibly around 100 AD. Here we find that the trial report is ten times longer than the original in Mark, and includes a whole new section where Pilate has Jesus transferred to his personal quarters and interrogates him privately there. Once again Pilate is reported to have said,

'I find no case against him.'

There are perhaps just two things in all the accounts of Pilate's supposed sayings at the trial, which are believable. When, in John's gospel he is approached by the Chief Priests who want him to change the sign posted on the cross; "Jesus of Nazareth - King of the Jews". They want it changed to read, "Jesus of Nazareth

- *claimed to be* - King of the Jews". Pilate refuses peremptorily, saying,

'What I have written, I have written.'

That sounds like the genuine Pilate, telling the Jews where to go, with no question of him rolling over for them.

The second is when he asks Jesus,

'Are you the King of the Jews?'

That was an unavoidable question, but not one where he would have meekly accepted Jesus' answer confirming it. That single point would have rendered everything that followed superfluous. In Roman terms Jesus had just condemned himself to death for sedition, and Pilate knew exactly how to deal with such people. It certainly didn't include any philosophical ruminations about the nature of truth, as reported so improbably in John's gospel.

Every single thing that we know of the man makes it clear beyond doubt that he would not have hesitated to condemn Jesus. Reported phrases such as, 'I find no case against him.' or 'I find no ground for the sentence of death.' are simply not the words of Pontius Pilate, the blood soaked prefect of Judea. This was a man who showed an unflinching determination, even at a risk to his personal safety, to put his subjects in their place; brutally and terminally.

As for his well connected wife, she gets just one brief mention in Matthew, where she promotes Jesus' innocence. Unfortunately, her words are no more believable than her husband's, in the end she's just another part of the pro Roman wall paper.

The reason why I have scarcely mentioned Pilate's appeal to the crowd about who should be released: Barabbas or Jesus? is because I don't think for a moment that such an appeal was ever made.

There is no record in any other source of this 'customary practice', nor is it believable that Pilate, of all people, would have ever allowed the crowd to determine something that he is said to have had strong feelings about. Either he didn't care about the outcome, which in itself negates the story, or he never asked the question. Having seen the man's character there isn't a credible third option.

In case anyone might think that Pilate was mellowing in his more mature years, think again. In 37 AD, about four years after Jesus' trial, following his lead role in another bloody massacre, this time in Samaria, he was removed from the governorship on charges of excessive cruelty, levied jointly by the Jewish authorities and his boss, Lucius Vitellius the Legate of Syria. He was summoned to Rome to answer these charges, and at that point disappears from history. Tradition has him banished to Gaul, where he committed suicide, but nobody really knows, once he reaches Rome the rest is guesswork.

Thinking him to be too good a scoundrel to pass by, I used a fictional version of his end in my book 'Barabbas'. In the real world he might have been a terrible governor and a vile human being, but he made a great villain.

The central point to bear in mind is not the date of the trial, approximately 33 AD, but the dates when the accounts were written, because that makes an enormous difference. The second half of the first century saw the accelerating shift away from *saving* the Jewish people, which had been the main focus of Jesus' ministry, and towards *converting* the gentiles.

This had started with Paul and his work in Damascus and Antioch, and then his series of missionary journeys. The original church in Jerusalem, under the leadership of James had, following the Resurrection, continued to devote its efforts towards the Jews, but the world was passing them by, they were becoming more and more marginalised. Even as early as the year 50 AD there were more followers of Jesus, what we would now call Christians, outside Palestine than inside it, and this difference was increasing every year.

This produced its own demands, what dietary requirements should be imposed on Gentile converts, and was circumcision necessary? Exactly the area where Peter and Paul clashed so bitterly. It also imposed an expectation on those people now starting to make the first written record of the church's founding years. The expansionist and evangelising wing of the church needed to use Roman infrastructure to travel to and from all these new churches that were being founded across the Middle East and in Italy, Greece and Egypt. Paul's missionary journeys relied heavily on Roman transport links.

This might not involve the whole hearted support of provincial Roman administrators, but it certainly had to avoid antagonising them. Added to which the acceptance, or toleration, of their presence in Roman administered territories provided a massive population of potential converts, men and women, freemen and slaves. So what could they do to encourage this acceptance?

You don't have to look far to see the problems involved in the unvarnished account of Jesus' trial. The Son of God, tried, convicted, flogged, ridiculed and crucified by Roman soldiers on the direct orders of one of the nastiest Roman governors in living memory.

This was a story that needed some work doing on it, several buckets of whitewash for the Romans, and the finger of blame pointed as firmly as possible to where it would do least harm - the group that no longer really mattered, the Jews. The basic details of who accused Jesus, and who executed him, were unavoidable: but a good deal of presentational skill could make things look better, and might even make them look acceptable.

The Jews had already turned down what was on offer, so the prize that was being played for now wasn't Jewish, but Roman opinion. A very high stakes game, and one that a lot of people thought it was worth cutting corners for. Political spin was not a twentieth century invention, it was probably around in Babylonian times; the reports of Jesus' trial before Pilate are just brief entries in a very long, grubby and continuing catalogue.

CHAPTER THIRTEEN

Mary Magdalen
- the lady vanishes

Unlike Judas and Pilate, the problem with Mary Magdalen doesn't lie in either her behaviour or her motives, the problem lies in her disappearance. We know that she and several other women, but almost always with her name mentioned first, accompanied Jesus on his ministry around Galilee. We know this from the fact that Mark, Matthew and Luke all tell us so explicitly. John is less directly explicit, but it is clear from the relationship he describes between them at the resurrection that they are, and long have been, close. The women, led by Mary Magdalen, are described as providing for Jesus 'out of their resources'.

If I were to describe Mary as being Jesus' road manager you might think me flippant, but that's not my intention. Jesus and the twelve disciples were the front of house performers, they were the talent, the headline act. They were the ones that people flocked to see, they were the ones with the news of the coming kingdom of God. But behind the scenes somebody had to deal with the boring stuff, the tedious details of where the food came from and where people slept at night, even the laundry needed somebody to do it.

When was the last time you ever heard a Christian speaker talk about how often Jesus' clothes were washed, or by whom? As I said, life on the road needs to be supported by a lot of detail work.

Jesus would often be invited to eat and sleep in local houses, but not necessarily everywhere, and how many local houses would have the food or sleeping mats available for all the disciples and hangers on as well. Somebody had to organise this, and it seems that somebody was a team of women led by Mary. From the reference to, 'providing out of their resources', it would seem this organisation also included paying the accompanying bills.

It would be a mistake to see this housekeeping role as purely menial, in so far as any society could at that time, Jewish society regarded the role of women as central, rather than subservient. This is why Jewish identity is passed down through the female line, it also accounts for Mary and Joanna being described as disciples. The fact that this allocation of jobs might not accord with our current preconceptions is just as likely to be our bad luck, as theirs.

There is nothing in Mary's reported demeanour to suggest simmering resentment, and nothing in her behaviour to make us think she felt herself held back in some way. They didn't know about our standards, and wouldn't have cared if they had.

The financing of Jesus' ministry is another of those areas, like the laundry, that is usually thought of as unimportant, it would somehow just *happen*. In my experience, very little in life beyond death and taxes can be relied on to just *happen*, somebody needs to organise it. Money would be donated by converts to

Jesus' mission, and in some cases by the grateful people who had been healed by him, but it wouldn't have been enough.

The essential point about Jesus' ministry is that he wasn't preaching to the rich and powerful, he was usually speaking to the poor and the dispossessed, the outcasts of society; it's a theme which crops up repeatedly. And, as in the story of the widow's mite, although what these people gave might have been a significant sum to them, it probably didn't add up to a lot in absolute terms.

There would have been a cash shortfall. It was this shortfall that women like Joanna helped to fill. She is named as one of the women who travelled with Mary and helped provide for Jesus. She was the wife of the steward to Herod Antipas, the ruler of Galilee, and it can be safely assumed that her high social status indicated wealth. Unlike the possibility in the British aristocracy of being nobly born but cash poor, the Palestinian model was more like the present American system; where social prominence equates to money.

In order to carve a path through the multitude of biblical Marys the gospels can sometimes seem to be packed with, unless I say otherwise, any Mary is Mary Magdalen. Despite what some writers have suggested, that does not include the Mary in the story of Martha and Mary, if you look at the differing Gospel versions and consider the surrounding details, it can't have been her.

The problem with Mary's story lies, as I said, in her disappearance. She appears fully fledged, almost from nowhere, as a close and intimate member of Jesus' inner circle, with the first significant mentions of her being at the cross, and then three days later, after the resurrection, she simply vanishes.

The one outstanding certainty about her is her central role in Jesus' ministry and life. She, above all the other disciples and followers, is unanimously named as the one person we can be sure was present to support Jesus at the crucifixion, the names of the others vary from gospel to gospel. Even Mary, the mother of Jesus, appears in only one of the accounts. The only other certainty about those present at the crucifixion is that none of the named male disciples was present.

The absence of the male disciples could perhaps be put down to their disillusionment at the death of their Teacher, because, despite his repeated warnings of what was going to happen, none of them really believed it. This is scarcely the first time in history that a regularly forecast event has come as a great surprise to those involved; the modern worlds of finance and politics sometimes seem to consist of little else.

Or, perhaps it was a prudent reluctance to avoid joining Jesus on a cross. Now that their leader had been dealt with, it must have seemed quite likely that the Temple authorities would continue their crack down on this subversive organisation, by moving to arrest the remaining senior figures.

I wouldn't call their actions running scared, or any other derogatory term, Jesus was several times reported to have changed his itinerary to avoid the Jews, in other words the Temple authorities. If Jesus considered such behaviour reasonable, then why shouldn't his disciples? It wouldn't have helped anyone at this time to see the remaining disciples in jail, or dead.

However, this leads us to a very striking conclusion about Mary, whatever the disciples' reasons for not being at the cross, she ignored them. If it was disillusion, then she was the outstanding figure who was not disillusioned. If it was fear, no matter how rational and well founded, then she was the outstanding figure who was not afraid. Or, more probably and even more strikingly, if she was afraid, then her love for Jesus was such that she ignored the fear and went anyway.

The same must fairly be said of the other women with her, even if we're not absolutely certain of the exact cast list, we know for sure that she had female companions.

One minor detail remains of the list of people present at the crucifixion, and that occurs in John's gospel. When Jesus was speaking from the cross John says that the, 'disciple whom he loved', was standing next to Mary his mother. None of the other gospels mention this 'disciple whom he loved', apart from John, who mentions this person six times at crucial points in the story.

The identity of this disciple remains unknown and it is not the function of this book to delve into that controversy, but I think it fair to make some brief comment. Whichever name you put forward for the role, there are a host of textual and narrative problems, none of the possible names provides a neat or easy answer. But the more closely you look at it, the more certain it seems to me that there can only be two serious contenders. First is John himself, the bookies favourite, after all it is John's gospel that provides the mentions, and secondly Mary Magdalen. She's the only other realistic option. Whichever way you look at the passion narrative, you always end up coming back to Mary.

The disparity in this story between the eleven remaining disciples and Mary is already large, and it's about to get larger. The crucifixion took place during the daylight hours of the day before the Sabbath, what we would call Friday, and Jesus' body was placed in the tomb that evening, just before sunset. That marked the beginning of the Sabbath, and meant that nothing further could be done to the body, by which I mean anointing it with spices and ointments.

The body lay undisturbed in the sealed tomb throughout the Sabbath, with at least two soldiers standing guard on it. It is believed that in compliance with Jewish law, none of Jesus' friends, family or followers made any attempt to visit the body during that time.

Although the Sabbath regulations officially ended with the appearance of the first stars on that evening, owing to the darkness there wouldn't have been much point in visiting the tomb until dawn the following day, what we would call Sunday morning. It is at that moment that anyone who wished to visit the body would have been able to do so.

Much can be made of the presence of the soldiers guarding the tomb acting as a deterrent to visitors, but they were there solely to prevent the body being moved, not to prevent access to it for funeral rites. The High Priests had been worried that the disciples might seek to hide the body and then claim that it had risen from the dead on the third day, as Jesus had predicted. Accordingly, Pilate's instructions had been that it should be guarded until the third day to remove that possibility. The only factors inhibiting visitors were those, already mentioned, that might have dissuaded people from attending the crucifixion.

It is, therefore, instructive to see who actually turned up. Once again, the only certainty is that Mary Magdalen was there. Matthew, Mark and Luke mention a varying list of other women accompanying her, whereas John says that it was Mary alone. We don't have to look very far to see a pattern in this.

I feel it worth pointing out that in all my consideration of the position of Mary in the Christian hierarchy, especially when you consider her central role in the drama of the Resurrection, I am making no comment on the historical truth of the Resurrection itself. Whatever you think of that, it has no bearing on the actions of the participants reported here. Whether the events occurred as described, and those involved did what is claimed, or it was all an enormous hoax perpetrated by the disciples, with those involved portrayed as doing what they would *probably have done*, doesn't matter.

The reason why, solely for this discussion, it doesn't matter is because either position gives us a direct look at the characters of the participants; either through their real actions, or through the actions that those closest to them could imagine them taking - and that's enough to work on.

The bottom line of my own position can be put most succinctly by saying that I am sure beyond doubt that it wasn't a hoax or a mass delusion. The actions of everyone involved argue very powerfully against that. All the direct witnesses spent the rest of their lives preaching about the risen Jesus and, in the majority of cases, suffering death on that account. Nobody would do that for a hoax, or a delusion.

If you want to look at a more subtle and reasoned view of the Resurrection than my own rather simple and direct approach, there is, needless to say, a massive bibliography on that exact subject. An interesting writer called Geza Vermes offers some very direct and accessible thoughts and possibilities on this and a wide variety of other biblical topics.

The events of those three days form the climax in the founding of the Christian church, the most intense set of events described anywhere in the bible.

All the battles and the kings and the prophets, and all that begetting - all forgotten now. King Solomon, King David, the Roman Empire, they all take a step back, to stand in line behind that one weekend in Jerusalem. The consequences of which are still being felt today, two thousand years later.

And who was there, whose presence was required to define these momentous events? Jesus himself, and the one other person who was second in importance only to Jesus. A person that Jesus clearly loved and whom he chose to represent, and stand in place of all his other followers, Mary Magdalen.

She is the one person we can name for sure who risked her own life to stand by him at his death, the one person we can name for sure who was there to see him resurrected, the one person he chose to speak to first when he left the tomb, the one person he chose to pass the good news on to the others. The depth and extent of their love for each other is unmissable and unmistakeable, it almost burns a hole in the page.

Even if I had some reason for wanting to, I would find it extremely difficult to downplay Mary's role in Jesus' ministry, death and resurrection, she is central, and yet she disappears. One moment she's there, centre stage with the action swirling around her. The next moment there's a flash and a puff of smoke, the trap door opens beneath her, and she's gone. How can that happen?

Allowing for the fact that the four gospels of Matthew, Mark, Luke and John are only trying to tell the story up to the resurrection, you can understand their lack of further mention. But that doesn't account for the complete absence of any sort of reference to her in the Acts of the Apostles, which is a straightforward continuance of Luke's gospel by the same author, and opens in the middle of the resurrection story. Nor, you might think, does it account for the absence of any mention of her in Paul's letters, which repeatedly refer to this period.

I am usually opposed to conspiracy theories, on the excellent grounds that they are usually rubbish, but this is almost enough to make me reconsider that view. To paraphrase Lady Bracknell; 'To lose one of your two leading characters in a weekend may be regarded as a misfortune, to lose both looks like carelessness.'

So far I have taken all New Testament accounts of Mary as being equally valid, but as with the development of the story of Pontius Pilate, as the writing of the accounts moved further in time from the events described, so the story underwent a significant change. The later the writer, the less importance is attached to Mary.

The original gospel, Mark's, written between 66-70 AD, is alone in awarding Mary the star billing. She is mentioned as the first name at the crucifixion, and at the tomb, and as the person telling the disciples. Mark is in no doubt about her importance. The term he uses to describe her connection with Jesus, was that she used to, 'Follow him and provide for him,' this has no connection with being a domestic servant. It is exactly the phrase used at that time to describe the relationship between a religious pupil and his rabbi, the pupil not only learnt from the rabbi but shared his daily life. Mark is describing Mary as a disciple.

In Matthew, Luke and John, writing successively between ten and thirty years later, her role is diluted to be one of a group of equals. You can see that it's impossible for her to be written out, her position is obviously too well known to too many people for that, but her unique position has been removed. As Matthew rather patronisingly puts it, 'Many women were also there, looking on from a distance.'

So far I have used only canonical sources, those accounts that were included in the present version of the New Testament, but there are lots of other sources, lots of other gospels, which for various reasons never made it into the New Testament and which vary in trustworthiness from good to awful. The individual slant that each of these accounts bring to Mary differs, the only fixed point being that they all refer to her a great deal more than the New Testament gospels, in fact the difference in the number of references is quite striking.

Their views of her significance and her relationship with Jesus cover a wide range. The Gospel of Philip, from the late second or early third century, suggests that their relationship was not only close, but sexual and might have included marriage, it also includes a question from the disciples, 'Why do you love her more than all of us?'

The Gospel of Mary, has been dated between Jesus' lifetime in the AD 30s, to as late as the early first century, as is often the case, there is no agreed consensus. In this a disciple is quoted as saying, 'Surely, the Saviour knows her very well. That is why he loved her more than us.' Exactly the same phrase used in Philip.

The Gospel of Peter from the mid or late second century, is generally unsympathetic to Mary, as might be expected given the name of the person in who's supposed authority it was distributed. It reports her function at the resurrection as being little more than an observer and messenger. However, even that gospel seems to let slip one significant point, when it describes her as, 'Mary Magdalen, a female disciple of the Lord.' In other words, not only was she a disciple, but more interestingly, it sounds as though she wasn't the *only* female disciple.

A third or fourth century gnostic (meaning, hidden knowledge) text called the Pistis Sophia is frequently quoted as being evidence of Mary's importance in the early church, as she is shown as the leading figure in a group of twelve disciples, made up of eight men and four women. However, being the dull plodder that I am, rather than just accepting that, I actually read the text for myself.

This turned out to be a frustrating and pointless waste of time The text is impenetrable, and its lengthy and intricate cosmology of gods, angels and extra terrestrial entities seems designed to defeat even the determined enquirer; presumably the reason for the term 'hidden knowledge'. It certainly remained hidden from me. Any quotes supporting Mary's prominence have to be very carefully extracted from the surrounding reams of arcane tosh. For this reason, as well as its late date, I place no reliance on its opinion of Mary. Look it up online if you're interested, and good luck to you.

Finally, and most instructively of all amongst the so called apocryphal gospels, there is the Gospel of Thomas, a so called Sayings Gospel, a non narrative collection of Jesus' sayings. This is another possibly early book, with dates suggested between 33 to 150 AD and, unlike the other apocryphal gospels, there is even a slight but conceivable chance that its first draft was actually assembled by its named author, in this case the disciple Thomas. It was a strong contender for inclusion in the canonical list, but it does requires a somewhat cautious approach, as several of the sayings are contradictory and some are no more than obvious and clumsy forgeries.

However, a careful and considered examination, weighing the feel and sound of the individual 'sayings', seeing how each one fits into the pattern of the others, how they are echoed in the New Testament and how inherently probable each one is, soon reveals a much clearer picture.

The most immediately arresting comment about Mary is in saying number 114, the last on the list, and apparently tagged on to the end as a later amendment. In this Peter allegedly says to Jesus, 'Let Mary (Magdalen) leave us, for women are not worthy of (the) life.' To which Jesus is supposed to have replied that he would make her male so that she could enter heaven.

This is such a bizarre suggestion and so unlike the other sayings, that it might as well have the word FORGERY written alongside it in capital letters. Not only is it wildly improbable in itself, it is contradicted by earlier sayings, (21, 61, 62) in which Jesus singles out Mary and Joanna as two disciples who are worthy of learning all mysteries, with no hint of a sex change being called for.

That's fine as far as it goes, we have spotted and discarded the forgery, leaving us with a clear statement of how highly Jesus valued Mary. But just hold on a little while, if you keep on looking, there is another layer beneath that, which is even more revealing.

Saying number 12 quotes Jesus as naming James (the Just) as his successor to lead the church, and that's unusual. Most of the other sayings are explanations or corrections, the only other individual named as being worthy of any special respect is John the Baptist, who is

194

in an entirely different league to James. This quotation doesn't come close to fitting in with the rest, it's a very square peg in a round hole. Furthermore, as soon as you pause to think about James' character and religious beliefs, it begins to look even odder. Number 14 argues against the avoidance of impure foods, saying that it isn't what goes into the mouth that defiles, but what comes out of it. Then in number 53, when asked if circumcision was necessary, Jesus replies that if it were useful then children would be born in that state.

James as a strict and orthodox Jew disagreed strongly on both points, a fact which would have been no surprise to Jesus who had known James all his life. These two issues were exactly the points which made James so unwilling to obey Jesus' direct instruction to make disciples of all nations.

You don't even need to rely on the Gospel of Thomas for this information, it's all in Paul's letters. And these facts make the possibility of James being chosen as Jesus' successor unbelievable, utterly unbelievable.

When you've established that this instruction is another of the fraudulent sayings, you need to ask exactly what its purpose was? During his time on earth, Jesus seemed to have nominated Peter as his successor; 'On this rock I will build my church', and the other disciples knew that, it was to them he said it. If Peter was still supposed to be the heir apparent then this subject needed no further comment or instruction, it had already been established.

The only thing that could possibly need further comment was if someone other than Peter had been nominated as successor. And that is precisely what this saying is all about, it's replacing Peter with some else. However, the presence of such a wildly improbable nominee as James is the strongest possible indication that a now unnamed third party was originally selected to replace Peter in the role of Jesus' heir, but that name was later changed. It seems apparent that the insertion of James' name in this way was an attempt to retrospectively justify his takeover of the Jerusalem church, some years after the event. All we need do now is decide who he replaced.

Nelson is famously supposed to have put a telescope to his blind eye, to claim that he couldn't see the signal ordering his retreat, and we would need to do the same here to avoid the blindingly obvious. If the nomination for Jesus' successor was being changed from Peter, who was it being changed to? Who did he love and trust, and who did he say understood his teaching? I don't even need to tell you, you already know.

The trouble is that no matter what Jesus thought about the irrelevance of gender in this context, both James and Peter disagreed with him, and they were there and he wasn't. The Jerusalem church elders, and on this occasion that includes Peter, were never going to accept a woman.

Consider, if you will, the real life, living breathing woman, at the heart of this mountain of comment, I have a mental image of her as I'm writing. The fact that there is no description of what she looked like, whether she was short, tall, young or old, doesn't stop the imagination or the semi educated guess.

In defiance of the almost certainly bogus tradition of her having red hair, we can reasonably assume that she would have been dark haired and more than likely brown eyed. She would have had a sun tanned complexion from a life spent mostly outdoors, and she would have been slim and fit, that's the only build she could have been: the work was hard and the food less than plentiful. As to her age, I think it impossible for her to have been older than Jesus, or else the stories of them being married or lovers would not have been so widespread. That puts her in her late twenties or early thirties at the time of the crucifixion. Was she good looking? The only clue to that is the fact that everybody noticed her, which I suppose is an answer in itself. I don't know about you, but I think that I would like to have met her.

What that leaves us with is the mysterious disappearance of a young woman who, to say the very least was one of Jesus' closest and most trusted confidantes, and probably a good deal more than that.

Were they married and did she bear Jesus' child? These are fascinating questions, but, as I said in another book; until someone turns up with a 2000 year old wedding invitation we shall never know. They were manifestly lovers in an emotional sense, but we can only wonder if, or how, that love expressed itself physically.

Try as I might, I can think of no reason why it matters greatly to Jesus' central role, although it is undeniably fascinating under that catch all category used by journalists: human interest.

If they *were* married, it would have been no more than a demonstration that Jesus was taking to himself humanity in all its forms, which, in other contexts, is just what he said he was doing.

What we can say with safety is that they were so close, and so much of one mind, and spent so much time together, that the answer to whether or not they were married is - they might as well have been.

Mary's removal from the New Testament record could have had several causes, though the way the gospel record changes with time, points very clearly to a growing antipathy towards her. The unsuitability of James to occupy the role of church leader, was because he was either unwilling or unable to see the wider picture. He couldn't see Gentiles as possible converts without erecting obstacles in their way, and he couldn't see a woman as his leader. Was there some kind of dirty tricks campaign to get him installed as church leader, ahead of at least two better candidates, or did he just have sharper elbows?

One thing we do know is that throughout history the first task of any usurper has always been to get rid of possible rivals. He repeatedly challenged and overruled Peter on doctrinal issues, and later, when Paul emerged as a powerful evangelist he did all he could to deny his importance. How sympathetic do we imagine this man, or his supporters, would have been to glowing references to a person that many people thought should have had his job? Mary might not have seen herself as his rival, but then she didn't need to, it was sufficient that *he* saw her as one.

I don't suggest that James was an evil or malicious man, he could genuinely have believed that his actions were in the best interests of the new church, and that neither of his rivals could offer the focus and determination that he provided in those dangerous times. Though from where I'm standing, he looks like something that's been left stranded on the beach by a receding tide; a strict and traditional old school Rabbi, quite unable to grasp that everything around him has changed, and he hasn't changed with it.

James' disagreement with Paul was even stronger than his rejection of Mary. Paul was not only a more successful evangelist, by a very long way, but was also sending urgently needed financial support from

Damascus and Antioch back to Jerusalem. Despite this James could never bring himself to accept Paul as being in any way his equal. It might be a frivolous personal comment, but unlike Mary Magdalen, I have never felt the slightest desire to meet James.

Not only is it the case that James would not have welcomed Mary's presence, or even her good reputation, it is clear from the biblical record that Peter himself was no more enthusiastic about her, he had dismissed her reports of the risen Jesus out of hand. This was a woman with powerful enemies. Whatever its other views on women, orthodox Judaism does not lend itself to female religious leadership, a point hammered home by every part of this story.

Yet considering her relationship with Jesus, it would have been difficult to relegate Mary to any sort of inferior position; far safer to push her out completely. This implacable hostility would have been more than enough to account for her removal from the subsequent record.

From a slightly different standpoint, one can see parallels in our own times, in court reports and newspapers. A rich man has died, leaving behind a second wife or mistress, perhaps justifiably well provided for in his will. His coffin is scarcely in the ground before the children of his first wife have have contested the will: he never really loved the second wife; she must have tricked him into naming her; she was only with him for what she could get; we should be his only true inheritors.

It's a story that's had a million replays, and one that I think Mary was on the receiving end of.

James and Peter, the leaders of the remaining disciples, thought that they alone should inherit Jesus' mantle, not some female interloper. This is why her reports of the Resurrection were so completely disbelieved, they were unwilling to award her the status they knew was her due, even when they must have known she was acting on Jesus' direct instructions. I have no wish to make St. Peter sound small minded, he was a lot bigger man than me, but in this case it begins to look that way.

One final suggestion to try and account for her vanishing act is even more simple. Perhaps she took stock of the latent hostility surrounding her and decided that with the man she loved, if not dead, then gone from this world, there was nothing left for her in Jerusalem. So she simply packed her bag and retired to the south of France, I've sometimes felt that way myself.

If Jesus did come again in glory to introduce the kingdom of God in her lifetime, it would make no difference whether she was in Gaul or Palestine, she would know about it and he would find her.

The persistence of the tale of her retiring to the place now called La Sainte-Baume, near Marseille, and living there for another thirty years, is so very strong that it's just about enough to overcome my normal distrust of folk tales. That story occurs so often and is so unvarying in its essential detail, that even without documentary evidence I think it's probably true. It would fit all the other known facts, it would account for her non appearance in the Acts of the Apostles, and as Paul was still years from writing his first letters, would account for him never mentioning her.

In contrast to my continuing dissatisfaction with the biblical accounts of Judas and Pilate, in the case of Mary I think we started with a mystery and have now probably arrived at an answer. At least I feel close enough to be satisfied, close enough to stop looking.

The only faint echo I feel is a desire to visit La Sainte-Baume, not to look at the place she lived, that's long gone, but simply to walk the hillsides she might have walked and to smell the same herbs, trees and plants that are, in many areas of that rolling countryside, unchanged from her day.

CHAPTER FOURTEEN

Sweet Charity
- a most toxic substance
where small is good and
even smaller is better still

Charity, even if it does begin at home, is surely a good thing. The sort of words listed in the thesaurus as synonyms make that clear; altruism, philanthropy, social conscience, benevolence, they leave no room for argument, it has to be a desirable attribute. But how pure is it? How pure can it ever be?

I'm tempted, for the sake of making a grand and sweeping assertion, to say that all human actions are, at some level, selfish. But I'm not sure it's true, we are back with that point about the difference between human beings and animals, some people and some of their actions can be genuinely altruistic. People do sometimes act for the good of others without any concern about the consequences for themselves.

Normally, the closer the beneficiary is to you, the more visible and thus measurable is the effect, and the more likely it is to happen. People tend not to sacrifice their lives for the good of society in general. However, I would remove from this category the act of a parent sacrificing their own life, health or wellbeing for their child's. Not that I wish to discount the act, it can still be noble and admirable, but I question the mechanics by which it occurs. I think that a parent's defence of a child, even up to the cost of the parent's own life, can often be mostly instinctive. I would suggest that it is rarely the result of rational consideration on its own.

However, to extend this level of attachment slightly, so that we include more distant relatives, friends, colleagues or military comrades, then we can find lots of examples of considered altruism. The soldier who throws himself onto a hand grenade which he knows is about to explode, in order to save his comrades. Or even more strikingly the volunteer health workers in third world countries across the Indian sub continent visiting deprived areas with polio vaccinations, of whom approximately 60 have been murdered in Pakistan on the basis that they are Western spies who are trying to sterilise Muslims.

But although such things are altruistic I think they should more properly be seen as bravery rather than charity. And anyway when it comes to bravery it's not me you want, you'd need to talk to an earlier generation; Margaret's father or my own father.

By charity I am essentially thinking of the donation of your personal time or money to a cause which does not directly benefit yourself. Under that heading I think that most, not all, but definitely most charity is to some degree self serving.

When you drop a coin into the Salvation Army collecting tin, you don't do it solely because you think this might help their work in tracing missing children, you do it either because you see it as somehow the 'right thing to do', or simply because it makes you feel better. When you send a cheque to the local hospice, or support a coffee morning to raise funds, it not only makes you feel better, but somewhere at the back of your mind is the undeniable consideration that you might one day need those services.

Or, the reverse effect of the widow's mite; when an incredibly rich industrialist donates fifty million pounds to set up a charitable foundation in their own name, did the absence of that fifty million pounds from their bank account have any measurable effect on their lifestyle?

Should I ever meet such a person, say at the wet fish counter in Sainsbury's, and even more improbably recognise who they were, my urge to congratulate or thank them for their philanthropy would be very small indeed. Giving away fifty million pounds is essentially a public demonstration that you can afford to lose fifty million, and not even notice it. That's not charity, it's advertising.

That consideration can and does apply at much lower levels. The man at a charity dinner who outbids all the rest to 'buy' a day's fishing, or something similar, is choosing to make a public display of his wealth. I don't claim that the charity doesn't benefit, but the principal beneficiary is still the donor, who has been paid in exactly the way he wants for the money given. In the same category is bungee jumping for charity, or bouncing on a pogo stick from Lands End to John o'Groats, these things are principally self aggrandisement with a lick of charity stuck on the end.

Reading back, I see this makes me sound awfully small minded - come on Ian, allow for a bit of give and take. But even if it's unpleasant to make such observations, I still think it's a fair and accurate statement of a slightly uncomfortable fact.

So if I'm that choosy about motives, what exactly do I see as pure and unselfish charity? How about this?

A good few years ago, when charity shops were a considerable rarity, rather than a high street commonplace, a young businessman met a regional director of the charity Oxfam at a social occasion. The man from Oxfam complained that despite several attempts they had never managed to establish an Oxfam group in a particular town, and how he was sure that if only they could get one started, it was just the sort of place that might raise serious money.

The businessman said that he worked near there, and was sure that no matter what had happened previously, he had sufficient determination to ensure that a local charity committee could be set up, and an Oxfam shop opened. Despite the Oxfam man's expressed caution in light of earlier failures, the businessman pressed ahead.

Advertisements were put in the area papers and a room was booked in a local pub to host the inaugural meeting. Through quite a lot of hard work and perseverance a committee was established and subsequently a brand new Oxfam shop was opened, which sure enough made good money. That sounds pretty charitable, there was no financial return for the businessman, in fact just the opposite, and where's the glamour or kudos in spending your spare time sorting through other people's cast offs?

That sounds like a good example in every possible way, until you discover that the businessman, as you might have guessed, was me, and that I don't have an altruistic bone in my body. So if I wasn't being unselfishly charitable, why did I do it - what was in it for me?

Two reasons; first, I'd boasted, while half drunk, that no matter how many other stumblebums had failed to complete the job, I could do it, because I was

Superman and I could do anything. It's embarrassing to recall this sort of attitude, but I was only young and I'm better now. It's one of the pitfalls of arrogance: that you occasionally have to come up with the goods.

Anyway, once I'd got started it turned out to be very interesting and there was an undeniable pride in watching the returns grow week by week. The second reason was that I was unmarried at the time, and a lot of the volunteers were good looking girls, wanting to know if there was any practical way in which they could express their helpfulness. So my payback was a boosted ego, a sense of achievement and an improved social life. Oxfam got something out of me for a couple of years, but I reckon I was well paid for the effort. There really are no free lunches.

Regrettably, in moral terms, I still hadn't quite cleaned up my act. Despite the fact that the shop was only allowed to sell items received as free donations, I reckoned there was a seriously good money making opportunity going begging. I'd seen tee shirt slogan printing machines in London, but knew there were none in our area and thought it could be a goer. I got hold of a reasonably priced second hand machine, bought in a stock of plain white tee shirts, and we were in business.

It was a fairly primitive early model and couldn't print the customers own pictures, just words and a small selection of preinstalled logos. We weren't fussy about the slogan, vulgar we liked, as long as it wasn't legally obscene or actionable we'd print it, and it made as much money as I'd hoped. Unfortunately someone at Oxfam heard about it and blew a fuse, so we had to pull the plug. We ended up putting the machine in the window and selling it on to the next budding entrepreneur.

The great majority of the people who come to our gun shop are reasonable sorts, people we're interested to meet and can happily chat to, but now and again we get another sort. People who have some kind of psychological reaction to the presence of guns, it makes them say stupid things, the most common of which is to claim that they used to be in special forces or the SAS. Our automatic assumption is that when anyone tells you they were; they weren't. If they really had been in the SAS they would probably tell you they were in the Catering Corps.

It's much the same with charity, the default position is that anyone who tells you they're motivated by nothing but charity is a bullshit merchant. (And they probably weren't in the SAS either.)

Whenever you read of B list celebrities plaintively wondering why everyone hates them, when everything they do is for charity, it's impossible not to think that life has moved beyond parody. I did part time work for a charity and was very well paid for it, not in money, but I was still well paid. It was a commercial relationship, which conferred no superior moral status on either party.

In a small aside about the Oxfam shop. For the grand opening ceremony I managed to speak to Ken Dodd and asked if he would consider opening the shop for us, he very kindly agreed, and said there would be no fee and he wouldn't even accept my offer of travelling expenses. But that was in a very informal conversation, six or seven weeks before the day, and whenever I tried to get hold of him nearer the time, I couldn't get through.

Eventually I convinced myself that he wasn't coming and so I rang the local mayor and asked him instead. Yes, he said, he'd be delighted and we fixed the date and time. On the Saturday morning, I had the bunting up, the press photographers ready and the staff in line to welcome the mayoral car; his honour stepped out with a smile on his face and his gold chain glinting in the sun. As I was welcoming them in, and his car was pulling off to go and park somewhere, an even bigger car pulled up on the pavement right behind. It was Ken Dodd, turning up exactly as promised.

I seriously considered trying to hide the mayor in a cupboard, if we'd had a vicar with his trousers falling down it could have been a Ray Cooney farce; but there were no vicars around and there wasn't a big enough cupboard, so I didn't think I'd get away with it.

I had to come clean and tell him what had happened, and that he was now number two in the running order, not number one. He was very good about it and said that he'd always been a fan of Ken Dodd's, had no objections to playing the straight man, and could I introduce them. It was a disorganised shambles but it seemed to work. It's as I've always told the children, when absolutely everything else has failed, you should at least consider telling the truth.

Moving back to the subject of charity; the ideal position, and one which I've never quite managed to pull off, is expressed in the old saying; 'Do good by stealth and then blush to be found out.' Or to approach it from a slightly different angle, you might say that public charity is always for an ulterior motive, but that private charity may just occasionally be pure at heart. From the sound of me I should change my name to Scrooge.

All the charitable situations I have mentioned so far have concerned charitable activity in this country, but that is only a part of the picture. A major component of charitable giving is for overseas causes; and I did say in the earlier section on prayer, that paying for a well to be dug or a school to be built can be more useful than simply praying for these things. But when it comes to overseas aid there are major problems of both fact and perception.

I have long had some sympathy with the suggestion that western aid to third world countries is an example of poor people in rich countries giving their money to rich people in poor countries. It sounds depressingly cynical, but unfortunately it also sounds true.

There are countless examples of financial aid being diverted to Swiss bank accounts, money that should have been spent on starving orphans being spent on private jets. But surely these specific examples of corruption should not be enough to damn the whole concept of third world aid, should they?

It would be nice if I could claim to be sufficiently broad minded and generous spirited to overlook this sort of shortfall, and if it was only the cash then it might be easier. The trouble is that the effrontery of the swindle is extremely galling to swallow, and the pot of available cash is not bottomless. But I still cannot envisage a world that is so self centred and mean that richer nations don't help poorer nations, in fact I wouldn't wish to live in such a world. However, it isn't just the fact that aid is being stolen, that is only a symptom of a more widespread problem.

I hope that I'm not straying too far from my brief here, this is supposed to be a book which acknowledges the miraculous and looks at some of the bases for religious faith from a non academic viewpoint. I don't want it to turn into a discussion on international relations, but I can't see how to discuss charity without touching on this huge and very visible area. So I'm going to take a slight historical detour.

In the same way that Muslims say, 'May his name be blessed,' whenever the name of the Prophet is mentioned, so the reverse is true with British educationalists whenever the words 'British Empire' are uttered. The phrase cannot be used in British schools or universities, or on British broadcast media, unless accompanied by some pompous imprecation about what an evil institution it was, and how it existed only to grind the faces of its citizens into the dirt. As is always the case with political slogan chanting, the reality was rather different.

Take, as an example, the country of Ghana in West Africa. From the middle of the nineteenth century until 1957 it was part of the British Empire. This is not some half baked micro state that you can drive across in half an hour, nor is it somewhere, like Northern Ireland or Palestine, torn apart by intractable ethnic disputes. This is a large and serious country with plenty of natural resources and a stable, civilised and well educated population.

Prior to independence, when they were all having their faces supposedly ground in the dirt, there was good road and rail transport infrastructure, an independent and non political civil service, an independent and free judiciary, universal free education and a thriving agricultural economy. It might not have been heaven on earth, but it was a reasonably well run, and successful country. In 1957 they achieved independence, after a completely peaceful transfer of power from the British, under their new President, Kwame Nkrumah. According to current political thinking this should have led to a flowering of increased political freedom and improved prosperity for all, as they were no longer having their money stolen by the rapacious filthy British. What actually happened?

Major parts of the agreed constitution guaranteeing personal freedom were ditched, detention without trial became commonplace, the judiciary and the civil service fell under political control and the economy collapsed. Personal incomes nosedived and standards of health care and even life expectancy dropped dramatically.

The only people unaffected by the collapse were the President and his cronies. Taking the most conciliatory view possible of this, let us say that the post independence debacle was caused by the British having failed to prepare them sufficiently for the rigours of freedom. If in doubt, blame the British, or even better the English.

Or let us say that it was caused by a wholly natural rush of blood to the head, which led to one two regrettable deviations from good government. If either of those possibilities were true, then the situation should have stabilised itself by now, more than fifty years later. To cut a very long story, with many possible examples, short - it hasn't.

Am I suggesting that Ghanaians are more corrupt than the rest of humanity? No I'm not, and that answer isn't prompted by ethnic sensitivities, I don't have any. The fact that they're black wouldn't stop them being crooks. In my own experience, Ghanaians and their near neighbours the Nigerians, both usually famed for their corruption, are not in actual fact noticeably more corrupt than say, Egyptians, Poles or Russians. It's no good you curling your lip and muttering, 'Well that's not saying much.' I agree it might not be saying much, but the situation I describe is usually about as good as things get with most nationalities.

Consider for a moment the fact that there are lots of impoverished countries, but very few impoverished leaders of such countries. That truism might be taken for granted, without a second thought, but it does summarise the fact that great power set alongside available money, produces a wholly predictable result.

What I'm trying to draw your attention to has nothing to do with national stereotypes, but something much more fundamental: human nature, and my low opinion of it; myself included.

My suggestion is that the inseparable twin tracks of political and financial corruption are so ingrained and widespread, that they might as well be regarded as the natural state of mankind, with disinterested honesty being the occasional exception. It looks as though, with one or two shining exceptions like Singapore, the only states to avoid the presence of significant and everyday corruption in their political affairs are those that have been democracies for centuries, and even there you will find periodic lapses, such as the British MPs expenses scandal.

Eliminating corruption is such a slow job that it is reasonable to ask whether it's actually possible. You can complain about the president's private jet, but you'll be wasting your time, the real point is that that's just the way the world turns, and you need to organise your affairs to take account of it.

There is a well known equation which applies to this situation, or is it an axiom? I'm not sure. There are descending levels of care and control exercised by people in varying spending situations. The greatest care is shown when someone spends their own money on themselves, slightly less care is shown when they spend their own money on someone else, even less when they spend someone else's money on themselves, and absolutely no care at all is shown when they spend someone else's money on someone else.

That last example is the situation with large institutional or governmental charity, a lot of pompous hot air and fine phrases, but in the end nobody really cares. It's all about being seen to do something, rather than doing it. As Lord Acton almost said: all charity corrupts, absolute charity corrupts absolutely.

Even at a national, rather than an international level, there are still problems. Two very large, old established and previously respected British charities, the RSPCA working on behalf of animals and the RSPB working on behalf of birds, have both been the subject of continuing and apparently well founded claims that many of their actions were politically motivated. And it is widely accepted that green and environmental 'charities' are little more than political campaigning groups. The whole area is a minefield, with the only certainty being the very noticeable lack of pure and untainted philanthropy.

Where does this leave my view of charity? I believe that not only is a great deal of charity, *to some extent,* self serving, much more significant is the observable fact that the larger the scale of the charity, the greater the potential target it becomes for fraud, and the more likely it is to be affected by political considerations, and thus corrupted. The problem is not principally the individual bent president building up his Swiss bank account, the problem is one of scale. There is a straight line correlation between size and ineffectiveness.

In the light of that, how do we then arrange international aid? I don't know for sure, but I wouldn't want to turn my back on the subject. The present arrangement manages to produce the doubly negative result of annoying significant numbers in the donor country and failing to benefit, to anything like the extent it should, the intended recipients.

As I'm sure the problem is one of size, perhaps part of the answer lies in reducing the size of the state administered aid budget, and in some way reallocating it amongst the private agencies. Caritas, Oxfam and Save the Children don't seem to run into the same problems as the state does. When was the last time anyone bought a private jet with Oxfam money?

But I don't think it's bad news wall to wall. Despite the permanence of our venality and corruption, human beings are capable of greatness in many more areas than that; science, music, literature, make up your own list, but whatever else is on it, that list should also include charity or altruism. No matter what I've said about the divided motives that so often accompany charity, there still exists a purity of intent in many cases, otherwise we would have no yardstick to measure anything else against. But I think the way to find that purity is by looking small and looking local, and very often it doesn't even involve money. Try looking amongst those people who would never be seen dead at a charity dinner.

In the New Testament, Matthew quotes Jesus, at the end of days, sorting the sheep from the goats, sorting who will be saved from who will not. Jesus condemns all those who saw him hungry but failed to feed him, who saw him thirsty but failed to give him drink, who saw him as a stranger but failed to take him in, who saw him naked but failed to clothe him, who saw him sick or in prison but failed to visit him.

The crowd, clearly shocked, ask, (I paraphrase) 'But Lord, when did we ever deny you any of these things?'

To which the killer answer is, 'Just as you did not do it to one of the least of these, you did not do it to me.'

For the sake of clarity it is worth observing that Matthew is effectively saying that when you buy a burger for the beggar outside McDonald's you are actually buying it for Jesus. I'll agree he's an unlikely consumer of a Big Mac, but that is what that passage means; just be grateful you weren't at the Feeding of the Five Thousand.

That might seem to be an almost impossibly difficult standard to live up to, you could devote your whole life to the pursuit of just that one goal, and still fall short. But as with so many other moral or spiritual injunctions, it is to be complied with to the fullest extent that *you can personally manage.*

To give food, drink or clothing to someone else, presupposes that you have these things to give in the first place, which in a modern society most likely means that you have a job and quite probably a family of your own. I don't wish to dilute the requirement, but such behaviour takes place *within* a normally ordered society, and not instead of it. When it comes to giving goods or money we can all only give from what we have already acquired.

However, that passage from Matthew also revisits a point I seem to have made once or twice already. When Jesus gave the disciples a prayer to use, The Lord's Prayer, it was very specifically focussed on a small and precise group of people; God, yourself and those immediately around you. In just the same way, when he offers an example of how you should charitably relate to the rest of humanity, his example is of the immediate and the personal. The man or woman standing next to you, or perhaps at one remove, and that's as far as he takes it.

This doesn't mean that you shouldn't send a cheque to Oxfam, or that you shouldn't support foreign overseas aid, because you should (whilst also campaigning loudly for it to be scrutinised a good deal more closely). But if you want to know where you personally can do most good, then it's probably within a mile or two of where you live, amongst people you already know. Alright, if you want to be picky, you can rewrite the last sentence to include that stranger you're supposed to be taking in, but you still know what I mean.

I'll give you a real life example of what I mean, something I've seen for myself, and you might have done as well. The middle aged woman who visits her husband's ailing mother in the care home, because her husband reckons he's too busy. She's never liked the woman, they've never been friends, there's nothing to inherit and she'll never be thanked by anyone - certainly not the old woman herself. She just can't stand by and see another human being left alone, unvisited and quietly desperate.

One day I might need somebody like that myself, I only hope I get it. Charity is happening alright, but it's low key, it's discreet and it's hardly ever actually called charity. I think true charity is like prayer, it works best when it's personal.

CHAPTER FIFTEEN

A Wider View -
and the Church of England's
strange reluctance to comment

After a large part of the book has been spent detailing my own shortcomings, and then what I see as faults in the biblical record, is there anything left for me to agree with? Which parts of my religion do I accept uncritically? Well, most of it actually. It just happens to be the case that it takes several thousand words to explain, in any sort of detail, why you disagree with something; whereas, uncritical agreement can be very brief.

Even when some of the more dubious peripheral stories in the New Testament have been stripped away, or at least heavily pruned, there is still a solid and convincing foundation to my beliefs.

Perhaps the most obvious characteristic of my Christian belief is it's relatively restricted reach, I'm no evangelist. I have never buttonholed anyone on the street with the demand, 'Have you heard the good news?' And furthermore I'm never likely to. This isn't because I'm shy, or that I have an excess of English reserve, it's more a case of it being a conscious choice.

Whilst walking through our local town centre to the bank very recently, I was stopped by a pleasant looking young woman carrying a sheaf of leaflets. Street canvassers normally avoid me, perhaps I don't smile enough or there's something unwelcoming in my manner, but this one pressed home her attack.

'Do you know what it is that you really want from life?' She asked.

Without thinking I replied, quite brusquely, 'Yes, a rich widow, with big bazookas, and her own pub,' and carried on walking.

Even though it's true that whatever she was pushing was probably of no interest to me, I hadn't intended to be so rude, that was just my instinctive and off the cuff reaction to being evangelised. If I unthinkingly react in that way to even a polite approach, then why should I think that anyone else would react differently? One answer might, of course, be that other people are just nicer than me. However, it could also be that thrusting yourself at strangers on street corners only works well for one particular profession, and I don't think it was hers.

I know that I probably wouldn't be a Christian myself, if it hadn't been for the death defying evangelism of thousands of brave and dedicated men and women, from Paul onwards. But that knowledge doesn't change my view of my own role in society.

As far as I'm concerned, now that I've finally cleaned up some parts of my own act, my Christian witness consists of living my life as honestly as I can, whilst letting it be known what my religious beliefs are. If anyone is then moved to think, well he's an OK sort of bloke, perhaps he's got a point, maybe what he believes in has some validity, then my approach has been successful. We can all only give from what we have within us.

If you wish to consider the other end of the scale, take a look at television evangelism. Margaret and I like America and we like Americans, and since we first went there on our honeymoon forty years ago, we've been going back regularly ever since. One time, not so long ago, we nearly moved to Wyoming, it was only the loss of contact with our children that stopped us. To summarise it roughly, we've been up and down both east and west coasts, along the southern border and done quite a few bits in middle. How's that for geographical precision?

The only major drawbacks are Hawaii, which we really don't like, and the strange fact that none of them can make cheese, other than that you can safely agree that we like the place. We even sometimes watch their television, despite the non-stop adverts.

But, as I say, for a real eye opener you should try watching some of their TV evangelists, they are spectacularly awful; crass, insincere, money grabbing con artists. Astonishingly, even though they regularly get caught with their pants down or convicted of fraud, the money seems to keep on rolling in. All countries have their national blind spots - and that seems to be one of theirs.

If such a thing were possible, they might have moved even further away from the evangelism of Paul in Damascus, than I have. If my approach, closely focussed on personal and private responsibility, lies at one end of the spectrum, then you may say that television evangelism is its exact opposite.

This prompts the thought that a lot of my views; on prayer, on charity and now on evangelism keep coming back to the same point: small is beautiful. I think that my area of influence in this world is minute, and that if I am to have any success I should tailor my expectations and actions accordingly. If I try to be of some help in the lives of those immediately around me, then I might have some small success. I don't want to ignore the rest of the world, but I should recognise my limitations.

For most of my adult life my primary role has been as a husband to my wife and a father to my children. They were at the heart of any duty of care that I owed to anyone or anything. When you expand that, you include my friends and neighbours, and the people I work with. After that, as with prayer, my effectiveness disappears and so does my ability to be of any individual use.

Looking at the role I seem to occupy in society, once I look beyond my family responsibilities, then my main concern should be to run my businesses in a way that is responsible and successful. I'm nobody's idea of a financial wizard or a business colossus, on a good day I'm distinctly ordinary. But what I can say is that no business I have ever been involved in has gone bankrupt or sought protection from its creditors, they have paid their bills and tried to be fair to staff and customers.

We have left no trail of broken promises or unfulfilled expectations, whenever I meet someone who used to work for us, it is always on friendly terms. I think this is because we have concentrated our efforts on our immediate responsibilities. Any organisation with a Corporate Mission Statement that mentions working for the benefit of the wider community is run by charlatans who will steal the shirt off your back. In fact you could change that to any organisation with a Corporate Mission Statement. What I'm talking about is the difference between useful practicality and empty rhetoric.

You may reasonably point out that our family businesses are only small potatoes, and I would agree with you. The most we have employed in any one company is twenty five, and it's a lot less than that now. But Britain, along with most other western democracies, is a nation of small businesses. The health, wealth and happiness of our society, along with the bulk of its jobs, depend much more on how well those are run, than on the management of shall we say Barclays Bank or Rolls Royce.

I'm not getting delusions of grandeur, and I don't think the weight of the world is on my shoulders, that's exactly my point, I have a very small and limited individual role to play and should concentrate on doing precisely that as sympathetically and well as I can.

In case you think that my ambitions are too restricted, I would respond that what some might call timidity looks more like realism to me. Far better for someone to do well, something achievable and useful, even if it is small, than to talk big and get nowhere. I don't want to teach the world to sing, no matter how many television talent shows might try to do otherwise. As Voltaire puts it, I want to 'Cultivate my garden', meaning that I want to take care of those people and things that I can see and reach out to.

On a related point, it might be worth noting that the average British Prime Minister, even today a figure with some authority and power, rarely manages to achieve more than one useful significant action in any single term in office. The more tightly focussed they are, the greater their prospective achievement, and that applies to the rest of us.

Returning to organised religion. The Anglican church, and particularly the Church of England of which I am a member, has long displayed a regrettable but undeniable reluctance to grasp certain nettles.

This might be seen as a useful counterbalance to rashness or impetuosity, if we're going to pronounce on serious matters we should consider our words before opening our mouths. No sensibly run organisation would wish to have me as its public spokesman. But there are some issues which have now been ignored for so long that our silence has become a statement in itself. That list has to be headed by, but is not confined to, abortion and euthanasia.

I have already discussed my views on abortion, and how I behaved when I felt my personal convenience and interests were threatened. However, my own failure in that respect means that all I could ever say to someone else on the subject, is that I hope their behaviour under pressure would be more honourable than my own. Scarcely a ringing statement of moral leadership.

None of this is any reason for the church itself to keep silent. It is not their role to pronounce on individual cases, but it might be hoped they could offer moral and spiritual guidance on important matters of principle.

To suggest that the present level of abortion in the United Kingdom is no more than an administrative detail and not worth bothering with, is a surprising display of selective blindness, if one were feeling especially sensitive it could even be described as cowardice. I can't attack anyone caught up in the realities of this issue, and wouldn't want to try; I don't even want to rehearse the pros and cons of the matter here. What I am saying, as clearly as possible, is that there *is* an issue here, and that issue has a serious moral dimension.

For the Church of England to say that they don't want to offend people by stating a Christian point of view is an abdication of their duty. The old phrase used to be, 'Publish and be damned,' perhaps in this case that might be changed to, 'Publish and be saved.'

Is it that we don't care? People are far more likely to abandon a church seen to be apathetic and frightened of its own shadow, than as a result of a clear statement of our position. Is our problem a fear of saying what we believe in, or the fact that we're not sure what we believe in?

You already know that I'm philosophically and emotionally opposed to abortions of convenience, you also know that a huge number of such procedures occur each year. If I'm so bothered about it - then what do I suggest we do? What I suggest is, that when caught in an offshore current it's usually best not to try and swim directly against it, but rather to try and go diagonally across it. You might not get back to the beach you started from, but at least there's a chance you won't drown.

The Church of England's position is comparable, we've drifted away from where we ought to be. A clear but compassionate statement of church doctrine would acknowledge reality and give some purpose to our presence in the public debate. We might not persuade everyone - we might not even persuade anyone, although I think we would, but our silence on this subject is abject.

Likewise, the Church of England's reluctance to tell certain other members of the Anglican communion, mostly African, that whilst we acknowledge the historical and even scriptural validity of their views on homosexuality, we no longer share them; because the plain truth of the matter is that we don't.

It would be a matter of profound regret if that caused their departure, or even the departure of individual members of our own church in this country, and I hope that it doesn't; but the possibility of such a split still doesn't change my views on the subject. Church unity is important, extremely important, and I would wish to increase that unity rather than lessen it. Even so, unity cannot take precedence over honesty. If you stretch the elastic far enough it will snap. Unlike abortion, homosexuality, whilst it might prevent the conception of life, does not generally lead to its destruction.

Even accepting the immutability of core Christian doctrines, we need to recognise that what we now call Christianity was an evolving religion even while Jesus himself was still walking the dusty back roads of Galilee. Take a look at his changing position on the desirability of Gentile converts. At one time he referred to offering salvation to Gentiles as 'Giving the children's bread to the dogs.' Yet by the time of his resurrection he was commanding his followers to, 'Make disciples of all nations.'

This was a man who looked about him and accepted the realities of his day, and then decided that the distribution of his core message was more important than the peripheral details, perhaps we should do the same.

I find myself to be both surprised and vaguely annoyed even to have say this, but I don't care if my vicar or my bishop is male or female, and I don't care if they're heterosexual or not. I do care that they should lead decent lives and be committed and compassionate human beings trying to spread the love of God, because

I've seen several that aren't. The fuss over homosexuality is a side show, and a side show that needs to be politely but firmly closed down - preferably now.

*****

The next bee in my bonnet, euthanasia, is a different kettle of fish, for several reasons. Unlike abortion or homosexuality, euthanasia doesn't generally come with an attached body of current practitioners, people who've been there and done it, and plan to do it again.

Homosexuality has been a feature of every society since the dawn of time, and abortion has been around in some form for just as long. In recent times, the only major variable in either activity has been the extent to which people were prepared to talk about it, or more commonly, not to talk about it.

This is not the case with euthanasia, it might have always occurred, but it was always on the margins, at the outer edges, rather than an every day activity. A deformed new born baby might be smothered; a dying old person might be helped along the way. But, at least in modern terms, it has always been a quiet, individual act, not a part of the fabric of daily life, not something that would ever need to be mentioned. A carer's conscience or pity, prompting an instinctive and often secret action.

This is why people react with surprise and disapproval when told of such, alleged, practices as the Eskimos leaving their old people outside the igloo to die in the snow. 'How primitive!' We mutter in the sort of shocked and prurient tones usually reserved for mentioning cannibalism. This absence of an existing group of self interested practitioners, following the departure of the deranged and murderous Doctor Shipman, means that the subject can be considered in an unusually open and frank way, working from basic principles upwards.

Almost all supporters of the Right to Die, as it is often called, choose to argue on the basis of some particular case known personally to them; inevitably a loved one who was forced to suffer great indignity and pain when there was no hope of recovery. A phrase used time and again is, 'If they were a dog, you would put them out of their suffering.'

But arguing from the isolated particular, to the wider generality, is a very poor way to approach any subject; to say that if a thing is correct in this one case, then it will be so in all cases, is hardly every true. This accounts for the continuing use of that well established legal maxim, 'Hard cases make bad law,' which is always true.

I accept that in the circumstances outlined above I might personally wish to end the life of someone who was suffering intolerably, with no hope of recovery, and I can also imagine wishing that benefit for myself, in a similar position. For me this is not, at heart, a religious issue, although as a Christian I respect the view that as all life is given by God, it should only be taken by God. But in my heart I know that if ever faced with a stark choice between avoiding sin or helping someone I loved, then I'm sure I would help the person I loved, it would be extremely difficult to justify any alternative to myself.

There is however, a major problem with such a position, and the problem is not with the theory, but with the practice. How often can you ever be certain, beyond doubt, that there actually is no hope, if not of recovery, then of useful remission? Sometimes, certainly, but not often enough to assume that all terminally ill patients are going to die when you think they will. That question alone, though not insurmountable, puts a serious stumbling block on the route to assisted death.

Going one step further, if we accept, as I do, that there actually are rare circumstances in which the suffering is appalling and all hope of any sort of recovery is completely gone, there is still more than one useful and merciful response to that situation. Instead of killing the patient, why not treat them? Not all treatment is aimed at recovery; palliative care is about the management of pain, the possible improvement of remaining life, and ultimately a dignified and pain free death. And that is where we come to the hospice movement.

Considering that one of the very few things we know for sure about this life is that we're all going to die of something one day, the management of terminal pain seems to be a surprisingly little regarded area. Hospices do their best, and Margaret and I have personal reasons to be grateful to them, but why should they need to be funded by charity? Is this really a part of our public service that should be funded by coffee mornings and the like? Why aren't these services supplied by, and an integral part of the National Health Service?

This is a far more pressing requirement for public funding than using our National Health Service to put rubber bands around fat people's stomachs. To help the weak willed obese might be a suitable cause for charity, relieving the intolerable pain of the dying is not.

To regard the decent treatment of the terminally ill as an optional extra, which might be nice if we could get round to it, is not simply a disgrace, it leads directly to the present situation where it has become acceptable to suggest that if we can't be bothered to treat the dying, we should just kill them instead. The more attention we give to this apparently well organised and vocal campaign to allow legal killing, the less attention we will give to providing proper care.

No matter how many tragic individual examples can be produced, it will never be enough to change the fact that we now have the technical ability to manage pain in all but a minute fraction of cases, and that with any sort of work on the subject, that could very rapidly become the ability to manage pain in absolutely all cases.

What we're talking about here is the requirement for the preservation of human dignity and the absence of pain, even acknowledging that in achieving that, death might come slightly sooner than it otherwise would. Perhaps, in pursuit of these aims, an amendment of the law is required allowing the dosage of drugs to be increased to whatever level is necessary, even if that does shorten life.

You might say this is coming close to the very thing I'm arguing against, but that would be to mistake the intent of the treatment. Managing death compassionately is not the same thing as setting out to cause it. It is surely not beyond our wit and intelligence to work out protocols for medical staff, which highlight that difference.

If the Church of England were to advocate some such direction of travel it might usefully combine practicality with morality, and would be a good deal more dignified than trying to pretend there simply isn't a problem to talk about.

What I've said up to now on this subject has been mainly from the point of view of the dying patient, and that is obviously important, but when you think about it, they are only one part of those who would be affected by a legally authorised Right to Die. To see why this is so, we can start by taking a look at events in the Netherlands, where such a law already exists, and the result is a very long way from any situation that I would be happy with.

The latest figures I can find come from a report in The Telegraph newspaper, which state that out of 4188 people killed by medical euthanasia during the previous year in the Netherlands, 55 of them were suffering from either severe psychiatric problems or dementia.

A variety of other cases are reported of doubtful informed consent, but as these are all debatable, and in some cases subject to legal proceedings I propose to ignore them. I want to look at just that group where it is not disputed that 55 people with some form of severe intellectual impairment were killed.

These are exactly the same category of people who, if they were female and a man had intercourse with them, he would be convicted of rape on the grounds that they could not have given valid or informed consent to sex.

So we have a group of people considered legally incapable of consenting to sex, who are somehow said to have consented to their own deaths. If there's anyone out there who thinks that makes sense, I'd be fascinated to hear their explanation.

Sadly, the people who are killed without ever requesting it are no more than the tip of this distinctly nasty iceberg. When the doctor arrives to make her rounds at the old people's home now, it is clearly understood that she has come to help people, if legalised killing is permitted that will change, for ever and for the worse. The unavoidable perception will be that she has a list, a list of those who won't be needing breakfast tomorrow morning, and that if you're not very careful she might put your name on it. I can't believe that is how most doctors wish to be seen.

How many frail elderly people, already confused and frightened, sometimes rationally, sometimes irrationally, will deliberately withhold information about worsening complaints or injuries? How many justifiable complaints of ill treatment or neglect will be stifled, on the fearful grounds of, 'Not wanting to cause any trouble'? How many inadequate and viciously disposed care assistants, and there have been countless examples of such, will routinely taunt their patients about the prospect of enforced death?

The very act of having to raise these points is deeply unsettling. Not a single one of your individual hard case examples, not even a whole raft of them, is sufficient to cover this point.

The stock answer to such enquiries is the glib assurance that such questions are no more than hysterical scare mongering, and these things would never happen in real life, to which I blow the loudest raspberry imaginable. Such things wouldn't just happen, they would become the norm, we are talking about opening the trapdoor to a very deep pit of despair and fear.

The suggestion is that everything will be safeguarded, and that no one will be killed without a form signed by *two* doctors, as if that made the slightest difference to the basic fact that killing sick people because you can't be bothered to treat them is barbaric. And remember, all those 55 mentally impaired people who were legally killed in the Netherlands had forms signed by two doctors - it didn't do them much good.

Whether you like the European Union or not is, in this context, irrelevant you simply need to bear in mind what the British people were told when they were asked to vote on that issue in the first referendum in 1975. All suggestions that to vote yes would be a vote for an all embracing European super state, were dismissed as hysterical scare mongering (how often that well worn phrase gets trotted out), in exactly the same way that reservations about legalised killing are brushed aside today.

When the Abortion Bill was introduced into parliament, opposition to it, based on the probability that it would lead to abortion on demand, was again dismissed in exactly the same terms. Assurances were given that this could never possibly happen, as the requisite forms had to be signed by two doctors.

Perhaps the two doctors they're talking about using this time are the same two endlessly compliant doctors they used last time, I think it's time they retired.

We haven't even covered the minefield of family pressures. The eagerly anticipated inheritance, if only the old bat would do the decent thing and die. Such things don't even need to be spoken out loud, the old person will assume that is what's being thought. These things are so often matters of perception. Even when it isn't true, the old person can still believe it; after all, they might reason, surely the government wouldn't have brought in such a law if it wasn't a reasonable way to behave.

I agree there's a problem to solve, and I don't think that all proponents of legalised killing are uncaring brutes, they're simply not very perceptive and quite unable to see further than the nearest 'hard case'. If they get their way we will inexorably find ourselves living in a meaner and nastier country, with a lot more suffering, not less. That is not a solution I want, it might not be a solution you want, and I cannot think it's a solution the Church of England wants either; so perhaps it's time they said something, rather than just allowing it to look as though they don't care. In the full knowledge that I'm repeating myself, I make the point yet again, to say nothing is a statement in itself.

The Catholic church in Britain has shown itself willing to discuss these moral issues, and to say where it stands, losing no support in the process. The Church of England, having nervously recoiled from difficult issues, has instead chosen the unedifying course of taking pot shots at easy targets, most recently the so called pay day lenders.

Fulminating about short term high interest lenders is a poor substitute for tackling abortion and euthanasia. Especially when the very misbehaviour these lenders are accused of, requires the active and willing complicity of the people they're supposed to be defrauding. People who often cheerfully admit that they lied to get the loans in the first place, and knew perfectly well they had no hope of ever repaying them.

Is such lending an issue? Perhaps it is, in a low key sort of way – but it's certainly no substitute for getting to grips with something as heavy duty and threatening as euthanasia.

CHAPTER SIXTEEN

<u>And It's Not Just the Church of England</u>

Whilst religious wars can't even begin to compare in their lethality and death toll with politically inspired killings, there have been an awful lot of them. Looking back through no more than European history, the awful truth emerges that there was never a time when somebody or other wasn't being persecuted for who or how they worshipped.

In sixteenth and seventeenth century France the Protestant Huguenots were almost constantly in a state of armed conflict with what there was of a central government, the death toll ran into the tens of thousands.

Although present day sentiment tends to see the Huguenots as the victims, the reality was somewhat messier; their doctrine was essentially Calvinist, and that is nobody's idea of conciliatory. Even that ghastly woman, later known as Mary Queen of Scots, makes a walk on appearance to encourage further killings. Obscuring the picture even further is the fact that a large part of the state opposition to them was not solely religious, but a dangerous mix of political and religious bigotry; which is, of course, the usual state of affairs, whenever conflicts are claimed to be purely religious.

Moving closer to home, in the British Isles. I don't think we need to trudge, yet again, through the tangled relations between church and state that existed in a particularly vicious way, from Henry VIII onwards, through the next two hundred years. A long historical view tends to soften people's rougher edges, and it's easy to forget that Guy Fawkes was the terrorist bomber, of his day. The murderous intent was every bit as strong then as it is now, but they were still working on the technology.

Underneath all that was the two thousand year old persecution of the Jews, running at differing levels of intensity all over Europe. Pick a European or Middle Eastern country at random, any one of them, and the question is never, was there persecution of the Jews? The question is, how much of it was there - and how lethal was it?

Some places had a sporadically better record than others, but no country had a long term good record. Christian countries condemned them for killing Jesus, and circulated such stories as the Blood Libel, which claimed that Jews used the blood of Christian children in their rituals. Muslim countries hated them on doctrinal grounds, with some sections of their teaching recommending their indiscriminate slaughter..

That wasn't even a brief overview of events, it was no more than an extremely restricted glimpse of two or three small areas. The point I'm making is that I accept, without qualification, the fact that religious conflict or persecution is every bit as nasty and every bit as endemic as the political variety. It is often the case that both sides of the equation, the victim and the tyrant, hold religious beliefs, which even if intolerant are at some level genuine. There is no moral advantage to the simple claim, 'I am a religious believer.' There should be - but there isn't.

The effect of this knowledge on me is to make me very cautious indeed about saying anything which might be thought conducive to encouraging such behaviour. I do not wish to promote or take part in any sort of religious persecution, but it's possible to be over cautious, it's possible to be frozen into immobility. We cannot allow a fear of overstating our case to back us into a corner, from which it is impossible to comment on injustice, for fear that someone may be offended. That would be intolerable.

A useful example of what I mean can be found in the area of race relations, we could look at any one of lots of countries, but I'm going to look at my own, Britain. For the last forty years or more it has been impossible to publically voice any comment about immigrants or immigration that was not wholeheartedly and unquestioningly supportive, without being branded a racist.

There was an astonishing view that immigrants didn't need to bother integrating into British society, and that they didn't need to learn our language, laws or culture. That they could and should stay in isolated ghettos, segregated on ethnic and linguistic lines, and that all state services, including health and education would be delivered to them through a massive system of state supplied interpreters. Thus, to use just one example, it became established practice that any white parent beating their child should be prosecuted, but a West Indian parent doing the same thing would be ignored, on the grounds that it was part of their cultural heritage. This idea was called multiculturalism, and it was the only view that could be publically aired without being howled down and denounced for thought crimes.

A man called Ray Honeyford, a highly experienced headmaster of an ethnically mixed school in Bradford, wrote a very mild and carefully worded article pointing out that this was not the best way to provide an education to immigrant children, or to prepare them for life in their new country. A tidal wave of manufactured outrage engulfed him, even his own employers decided that they couldn't stand by him. Despite the excellence of his record and the modesty and complete accuracy of his comments, he was forced out of his school and never worked again. His very name was turned into a byword for intolerance, by people who had never raised a finger to educate anyone in their lives.

That is where we find ourselves when we spinelessly surrender the public arena to demagogues and fanatics, on the grounds that we don't want to be called racists, all rational discussion is made taboo. As far as race is concerned, it is, at long last, becoming politically acceptable to cautiously raise the fact that multiculturalism was a disastrous mistake, which for decades damaged immigrants chances of integration and poisoned the well of race relations. You would think that was a good thing, and it ought to be - sanity returns, long delayed, but better late than never.

Unfortunately, the very same class of people who enforced the rancid shambles of multiculturalism have now turned their attention from race relations to religious relations. In the same way that education has for so long been subject to the attentions of people who seek to merge education into indoctrination, so now religion is to be overseen and in some way validated by people who wouldn't go in a church if you paid them. People who think the pulpit a suitable place from which

238

to disseminate their current political message to us punters in the pews.

All the usual suspects are there: the metropolitan political elite who have never worked in anything but politics, the hierarchy of the BBC, race relations professionals, most senior clergymen and a great many senior police officers. Common factors they share are their separation from the daily lives of 99% of the population and the fact that there is no visible connection between their pay and any measurable output.

The presently fashionable posture that all these people so wholeheartedly agree on, is that Islam is a good and peaceful religion, which just happens to have a few bad apples, a small number of hotheads at its fringes. One begins to wonder if they're right; they say it so often and so loudly, but then you remember their dishonest and disastrous track record on race relations and caution returns. Besides which, the extremely shifty and evasive way in which this subject is being handled would, on its own, be enough to make you disbelieve them.

No matter how objectionable some aspects of Muslim behaviour might be; the only correct response is supposed to be a pretence that it isn't happening, or that if something is happening then it has no possible connection with Islam. The cry is, 'Why are you demonising Muslims? Why don't you look at bad behaviour in the white or Christian community?'

However carefully you approach this subject, or from whichever angle, as soon as you arrive, you're told that you have no right to be there. This does no service either to Muslims or to the rest of us. If it's really true that the problem is no more than there being a few bad apples in the barrel, then surely the sooner they are identified and dealt with, the better for all of us.

However, the disturbing and growing possibility, that we can no longer ignore, is that it might not be a case of a few bad apples, but of something intrinsic in the religion itself which is causing the problem. Does Islam possess attributes which make it unsuitable for a pluralistic society, for a western democracy? Are there beliefs integral to Islam that do not accord with personal freedom and sexual equality? When the question is posed as starkly as that, the answer is quite clearly, yes.

What I'm talking about here is not immigration per se, nor even the large numbers involved, even though those are both perfectly proper and legitimate topics for discussion, but rather the essential nature of a particular immigrant group. This whole subject is shrouded in so much denial and evasiveness that even to look in this direction is to risk the most gross abuse, but we, as a society, should not be deterred. If there are problems of compatibility they need to be recognised and addressed, then, and only then, is there the slightest prospect of dealing with them.

Clearly this doesn't apply to all Muslim immigrants, but it is much more than a matter of, as with non Muslims, that some of them are nice and some of them are nasty. The problem goes beyond the natural and random spread of nastiness in the population, which affects us all; there is a visible and active part of the Muslim community which is determined not to integrate, and for whom no accommodation will ever be enough. The demand for Sharia law today, the demand for 'no go' areas for patrolling police officers tomorrow.

These are people who not only don't have the slightest intention of adopting British standards in either their private or their public lives, but believe they have the right to oblige others to adopt *their* standards. They believe the tail should wag the dog.

An everyday example of this lies in the censorship of public comment about their religion, a censorship which applies to no other group, religion or nationality. The BBC and most newspapers now censor themselves on this subject for fear of the inevitable death threats that will follow any 'disrespect'. This, it needs to be remembered, is an area where the word 'respect' is entirely synonymous with the word 'fear'.

Quite alarmingly, some prominent universities have allowed themselves to be bullied into accepting gender segregation in the audiences for guest speakers, claiming that they were doing no more than acceding to student requests. Even Oliver Cromwell, at his most puritanically strident, never tried pulling a stunt like that. This sort of coercion is alien to our culture and should have no place in our society.

Even less creditable in our seats of supposedly higher learning is the overt anti Semitism, which is now so routine and widespread that it usually passes without comment. Vainly attempting to use the wholly transparent fig leaf that their actions are anti Zionist rather than anti Jewish, all sorts of restrictions and prohibitions are imposed on reciprocal contacts with Israeli institutions and Jewish speakers. This is not because of anything they have individually said or done, but simply because they're Jewish, that alone is more than enough to damn them.

The fact that Muslims are free to live their lives and practise their own religion in Israel and Britain, quite unlike, for example Jews and Christians in Syria,

Saudi Arabia, Afghanistan, Somalia, Yemen, Sudan and so on, seems to be irrelevant to these brave upholders of academic freedom.

The country of Israel is a long way from perfect, but to compare it with any of its undemocratic and repressive neighbours, and then decide that you wish to ingratiate yourself with, and suck up to those neighbours, makes absolutely no sense at all. Mind you, hearing that the some British university wants to prohibit all contact with the country that has won more Nobel prizes per head of population than anywhere else in the world, is a bit rich. It reminds me of that old newspaper headline, 'Fog In Channel – Europe Cut Off'.

I recently read a description of anti Semitism that might be appropriate here; it's the noise you hear when lazy stupid people whine about hard working intelligent people.

However, that's quite enough about academic bigotry, I want to return to the more pressing problem of the unwillingness of certain Muslims to integrate into British society.

It is uncritically accepted that a disproportionate number of any racial group in prison is, in itself, proof of an injustice, a proof of systemic racism. But what if such a disparity were no more than a reflection of the gap between that group's interpretation of their religious or cultural beliefs and our society's values? Should we adjust our criminal justice system to convict fewer felons once that group's racial quota has been reached?

In the case of these particular Muslim immigrants to the UK, I am unaware of any short cuts to identifying this non intergrationist group by the use of simple labels. They aren't exclusively Sunni or Shia, nor are they easily split into traditionalists versus modernisers, or even young versus old. The best way that I can express it is to say that these are people who believe that their religion, and their social values, should not simply influence or inform society, but completely dominate and control it.

This isn't something historically unheard of in Christian societies, I would just remind you that wherever it has been tried, it has been a disaster, and that will be as true for Muslims as for Christians. That said; the only realistic means of identifying these people today seems to be by their actions. I offer the following as possible examples of this mindset.

There have been several recent cases of Muslim men, usually of Pakistani origin, grooming and sexually abusing, young white girls. For years these cases, although well known to the police, had been ignored on the grounds that it might damage race relations to investigate them. When newspapers describe these events, the offenders are euphemistically referred to as 'Asian', as though they might be Chinese or Korean. No one is fooled by this, but a lot of people are exasperated by the stupidity of the evasion.

The public is repeatedly and vehemently told by politicians and television commentators that this is not a racial issue, and that most sexual abusers of children in the UK are white. Whilst this is undoubtedly true, it ignores the vital point at the heart of this issue which is that when it comes to the abuse of vulnerable young girls, Muslim men are significantly over represented in terms of their presence in the population.

That is the precise point that public discussion of this subject never wishes to address, it is always allowed to slide evasively away, like trying to grasp wet soap in the bath. This means the only people with a public platform prepared to oppose this view are populist tabloid newspapers; a deeply unsatisfactory state of affairs. Thus it can be spuriously claimed that, 'This is just some story whipped up by the Daily Mail.' (You will note that it's always said to be the Daily Mail, I swear I'm going to start reading it one day.)

Though this abuse is predominantly a sexual crime against the victims, it is also a social crime against society, and has surfaced in so many different areas that it is fair to see it as a generalised statement of their rejection of British values and laws. Quite correctly, no such immunity from public comment was ever granted to sexually abusive priests, with answers and action being demanded from the Archbishop of Canterbury and the Pope. The unwillingness of the police to investigate, and of public figures to address the issue, seems restricted to Muslim occurrences.

Voter fraud in United Kingdom elections can be perpetrated by people of any ethnicity, yet once again, it is in practice an offence committed primarily by first and second generation Muslim immigrants. I do not believe that if we ever bothered to catch, convict and imprison such people, it would be reasonable to call that racist. I would call it something more like justice.

Unlike female genital mutilation, which apologists attempt to excuse as being a cultural hangover from the 'old country', albeit an extremely nasty one, voter fraud doesn't even have that excuse. It is straightforwardly criminal. When my own actions were criminal, I was well aware of the fact, and so are these people. There are no cultural excuses.

Honour killings are not honour killings, they are cowardly killings. The victims are almost exclusively young women and the killers, although again not solely Muslim, are disproportionately so. This, more than any other action, seeks to turn women and girls into possessions, into objects to be bought and sold for dowry, and where necessary, disposed of like so much unwanted rubbish.

Are we to say that these are just more of the sort of offences carried forward as cultural baggage from their background, or is it Islam which encourages a view that women are lesser creatures?

Once you adopt such a viewpoint, it is a very short step for the weaker and more feeble minded men in that community to imagine they have the green light for abuse and murder. Especially so, when in the case of child grooming, the victims are 'kuffars', or infidels, as they choose to call their fellow citizens.

Even the simple use of such a word would be prosecuted as a hate crime, if used by whites about blacks. Yet scarcely a hand is raised against them, either by their own community, or by social services, nor with sufficient force by the police.

First cousin marriage was a bad idea when it was practised by European royal families, and had damaging genetic consequences for their offspring. It is still a bad idea now and continues to offer significantly increased prospects of damaged children. Now that royalty have moved on, this is largely a Muslim activity with something like fifty percent of Pakistani origin British Muslims marrying their first cousins. Do we seriously believe this to be a benefit to our society, to any society?

Such marriages, inevitably organised by the parents, and the examples I quoted of criminal behaviour, are displays of the male control of women. Even in the case of voter fraud, which might have seemed immune to that charge, the standard practice, at its simplest, is that the male head of a household will fill in postal voting cards for his wife and voting age daughters.

The most obvious exception to this pervasive anti female pattern would seem to be the abhorrent belief that homosexuals and apostates should also be murdered. But I would hardly call extending your death list any sort of an improvement.

It is accepted that other ethnic and national groups engage in every sort of criminal activity; individual white British Christians are perfectly capable of being every bit as nasty and criminal as individual immigrant Muslims; but that's not the point. The point is that there is a visible and repeated *pattern* of criminal and socially corrosive behaviour which should have no place in our society, and which is statistically over represented in the Muslim community.

I regard it as self evident that residence in the United Kingdom comes with certain minimum requirements of social compatibility. We used to burn witches in this country and hang small children for stealing handkerchiefs, but came to recognise this as barbaric and so stopped doing it. There are some aspects of the non integrationist strand of Islam which urgently need to make the same discovery.

Even accepting the welcome cultural variety that Britain has assimilated with its immigrants, there is a more pressing moral difficulty with religiously separate incomers. Every religion will have its own sticking points between it and a wider secular society, including Christians. Yet Hindus, Sikhs and Jews and, since the Reformation, Catholics, had exactly the same dilemma to resolve, is your primary allegiance to God or Caesar?

The fact that all the other groups have managed this doesn't imply they take their religion any less seriously, it just means they're more realistic and more

246

mature. It means they prefer to live in peace with their neighbours, rather than kill them.

The longer we continue to ignore this subject the harder it will be when it eventually turns round and bites us, which it undoubtedly will. Vaguely yearning to live in a stable and balanced society, where we all obey the same laws, is comforting but pointless, unless we're prepared to take some steps to get there.

Unfortunately, 'all the usual suspects' I identified earlier, the insular metropolitan elite, won't touch this with an extremely long barge pole – but somebody needs to. Without being alarmist, it is doing no more than stating the obvious to remind you that the suicide bombers are already here, and people are already dying on British streets.

Although certainly offensive and probably inaccurate, it has become an accepted social and medical cliché to say that a lot of the men dying from bowel and prostate cancer have only themselves to blame, because they were too embarrassed, or too thick, to visit a doctor at the first symptoms. Whatever the truth of that, we seem to be experiencing exactly the same sort of lethal reluctance to get to grips with the issue here; to deal frankly and honestly with this perceived incompatibility between some Muslim expectations of society, and those of the bulk of our existing population, whatever their origin. I can only hope the result of this neglect is not similarly lethal.

Some part of our problem in facing up to this incompatibility and to actual terrorism itself lies in the growth of a culture which equates perceived offence with actual injury. Suggesting that an obese person might help themselves by eating less is seen as an attack on their human rights.

Publically stating that your religion regards some forms of social or sexual behaviour as reprehensible is now a legally defined hate crime that can and will put you in a police cell. That is surely unacceptable. Such statements, made by any religion, should be part of the normal give and take of public life, you can listen to them, you can laugh at them or you can call them rubbish – but unless they are advocating violence or repression, you should not be able to prohibit them. The basic premise here would seem to be – grow up and get a life - which is the exact opposite of suggesting that human life should be free of anything you might find challenging.

With that in mind, Muslims should have exactly the same rights as Christians, or any other group, to publically state their beliefs – no matter that others might find them offensive. The problem arises when some group only wants to accept half of that equation, they want the right to offend others but then say they will kill anyone who offends them.

The idea that some people should not only take such a demand seriously, but even wish to appease it is astonishing. Nonetheless, this attitude was in evidence after the recent cowardly murders of journalists and cartoonists, carried out by militant Muslims in Paris. BBC Radio broadcast an interview with a woman who, after some perfunctory bromides about how she deplored all killing, delivered herself of the opinion that whilst freedom of speech was, of course, a good thing, it must never be used to cause offence. Journalists, she said, should be forced to use their right to free speech solely to build bridges between communities, particularly with Muslims, as killing people in response to a perceived insult was, 'their way of dealing with things'.

That this sort of drooling imbecility can be passed off as rational comment by our state broadcaster leaves me wide eyed and shell shocked. My concern is that this woman was not alone in her eagerness to abandon hard won freedoms, and that such sentiments will offer more encouragement to the next bunch of killers.

For once, however, my main complaint here is not about the Church of England's unwillingness to speak out; although that sound I can hear in the distance is probably a lot of clerical feet running for cover. Added to which, there is the point that if we don't want to comment on a subject combining morality, religion and the cohesion of our society, then I do wonder what will we comment on?

No, I think this is initially and primarily a responsibility of the Muslim community. Effective action by the wider society would almost certainly have to be in some way repressive, and although that might become necessary, it isn't the best starting point.

Christianity and Judaism have both gone through periods of internal strife and blood letting, and it seems that Islam is undergoing something similar at the moment. More of the current problems in the Middle East are caused by one sort of Muslim hating another sort of Muslim, than any sort of Muslim hating either Christian or Jew.

It is also true that we should be involved in fewer military adventures far from home; to misquote Bismarck, all the problems of Afghanistan, Iraq and Libya are not worth the bones of one Lancashire Fusilier. Even in those instances where some kind of democratic election process is engineered, the results are no improvement. The rare examples of free elections in Muslim countries usually return governments intent on killing people they don't like..

However, none of our interventions in Arab politics, disastrous and pointless though they inevitably are, can be held responsible for the rejection of our culture we see so prominently in some Muslim immigrants. At best such flag waving escapades do no more than provide a convenient peg, on which they can hang their pre-existing contempt and hostility for the host nation and culture.

I have the feeling that a lot of Muslims go through their lives in exactly the way that I went through so much of my own. They see occasional examples of criminal or unpleasant behaviour by those around them, in this case their fellow religionists, and find it easier to avert their gaze than do anything about it.

It will be difficult to bring about the necessary change in their culture, whereby criminal behaviour within their own community is reported to the police, rather than being fearfully ignored; and I accept that in this, as in so many other areas, I have little room to give lectures. But unless such a change of culture occurs, I can't see any realistic way of producing a unified and peaceful society.

That is why I believe that the wider Muslim community need to recognise that there is a genuine problem that needs to be dealt with, it isn't just newspaper scaremongering, and cannot be dismissed as racist. There is one particular part of their society which doesn't want to live at peace with their fellow citizens. A good starting point would be for them to acknowledge that's where the problem lies, and not with some litany of imagined offences they claim to have been subjected to.

Islam has a problem that needs to be addressed, and trying to claim that anyone who mentions this is *Islamophobic* doesn't help. The first and unavoidable step in dealing with any problem is to acknowledge that the problem exists.

I cannot help but believe that a degree of clarity in this area would be even more beneficial to the majority of Muslims than it would to the rest of us. It seems to me very obvious that, to take just one example, Muslim men who don't rape young girls would not wish to be lumped together with those who do. Yet they are the only people who can introduce that visible distance between them, I just wish they'd get on with it.

CHAPTER SEVENTEEN

Allegiance and Loyalty
- the tangled web

The unavoidable problem with religious belief in any secular society is how those two responsibilities meet; where exactly is the dividing line? An accusation historically levelled against the Jews has been that they owe their allegiance to some concept of international Judaism, and not to the nation state they live in; thus meaning their loyalty can never be relied on. In Britain, exactly the same charge has been made against Catholics for at least the last 500 years; they served the Pope and not the King, they were potential traitors to our national interest. Now the question is being asked, amongst others – by me, of Muslims.

The dangerous potency of this charge is not that it's a load of nonsense, but that it contains some elements of truth that attach to all of us.

I acknowledged in the last chapter that there was, or at least could be, a problem of divided loyalties, and said that those with strong religious beliefs who had resolved this were not being irreligious, but realistic and mature. Moving away from solely Muslim concerns, it is worth a few paragraphs to look at this in a wider context.

I feel enough of this possibility within myself to appreciate the dangers. I have already made it clear that immorality bothers me far, far more than illegality, and that's the only thing necessary to place you firmly into the middle of this dilemma. Though frankly, I'm in the awkward position of having form in both areas; immorality and illegality.

One of George Bernard Shaw's famous exchanges occurred at a formal dinner, when he asked the woman next to him if, recognising the huge amount of public good she could do with the money, she would sleep with him for a million pounds. After very little hesitation she replied that it would be her public duty to do so. He then asked her if she would sleep with him for five pounds.

'What do you think I am?' She asked, outraged.

'We've already established what you are, all we're doing now is haggling over the price.'

As it was with that lady, so it is with the moral divide between church and state; deciding where to draw the line between two conflicting imperatives. Once you admit the question has any validity at all, and it clearly does, you find yourself not just with a problem, but also the possibility of deliberate trouble making. It's easy enough to come up with examples of evil or misguided behaviour on this point.

In the seventeenth century a plausible rogue, Titus Oates, produced supposed evidence of a Popish Plot to kill Charles II, which preyed on legitimate public fears of a Catholic invasion. This produced a good deal of hysteria and resulted in a great many innocent men being executed, and yet was based on nothing but fantasy. The fact that some group in society has a moral choice to make about their primary loyalty, leaves the way open for unscrupulous rabble rousers to foment trouble for their own ends. The problem is that even knowing that, it doesn't prevent the accusation of disloyalty from occasionally being true, which is why it's such a complex subject.

It isn't just religious divides that present this problem. Three centuries later there was a cell of communist agents in the British security services, from the 1930s to the 1950s, largely based on a Cambridge group of idealistic, and mainly homosexual young men calling themselves The Apostles. They seem to have genuinely believed that the supposed moral superiority of Russian communism took priority over the interests of their own country. Unlike Titus Oates, they weren't responsible for tens of deaths, but for hundreds and possibly thousands of deaths.

In yet another of my little diversions I think it worth pointing out that the existence of this self regarding group at the heart of the British intelligence community was quite widely known, and apparently accepted as in some way 'normal'.

My father, who had ended his wartime Military Intelligence service in an outfit called MI19, was the subject of a persistent and determined attempt to recruit him back into MI6 after the end of the war. His refusal, though actually based on his desire to return to the family business, was bluntly expressed to his MI6 contact, an unconventional and interesting character called Johnnie Ray, in the following words, 'I wouldn't get into bed with that bunch of back stabbing effing nancy boys if you paid me in gold bars.' Whatever was happening in MI6 was hardly a state secret, yet it took another ten years before it was publically exposed.

Also a product of the 1930s is the well known comment of the novelist E.M. Forster on this same subject, 'If I had to choose between betraying my country and betraying my friend, I hope I should have the guts to betray my country.' Which I must confess leads me to think that perhaps Mr. Forster should stop being so theatrical and choose his friends a little more carefully.

My own view is that whilst the problem undoubtedly exists, it is in reality a dead end. In the same way that the question, 'Have you stopped beating your wife?' is a linguistic trick, so the church/state divide on grounds of conscience is a philosophical trick. The answer is that there is no answer to fit all occasions, this is an area of shifting sands and any idea of drawing firm dividing lines is a non starter.

We're human beings, flawed and fallible. Faced with a set of circumstances one day, you might reach some particular decision, but faced with the same circumstances the next day, or if feeling tired or irritable, you might reach a different decision. Human affairs are messy, it's in their nature.

This is one of those parts of life where you simply have to muddle your way through, as best you can, and if you find that unsatisfactory, then perhaps you should adjust your expectations of life. Could a Catholic, a Jew or a Muslim be trusted to act in the interests of the state if they felt a moral conflict? I already know there might be circumstances where you couldn't trust me, but what about you? And how about them?

Sometimes the question might involve relatively minor points, the sort of thing most people would shrug off, but at other times, as in 1930s Britain, it could well be the vital national interests of the state. But the seriousness of the outcome doesn't change the nature of the question.

Could you trust a Catholic, can you trust a Muslim? It depends on the Catholic, it depends on the Muslim, and it depends on the circumstances. The first Queen Elizabeth said that she had no desire to make windows into men's souls, and neither, at a less exalted level, do I. This means that while I still believe we must all accept the rule of common law, I will never be able to answer this question definitively, I'm not even sure that I want to. A little uncertainty keeps us all on our toes.

*****

At the time of writing this book, there is a degree of public disquiet and fear over the issue of young British Muslim men going off to foreign climes to fight for various Islamic groups, the most recent being a psychotic bunch of medieval barbarians calling themselves Islamic State. More than the indignation at this perceived rejection of our society's values by people who were born and raised here, there is a much greater fear of what these people might get up to, if ever they return to Britain.

I don't discount or belittle this fear, I think it perfectly reasonable to discuss what our reaction should be to such hostile and dangerous people, who in many cases will actively wish to harm us and our society. I don't have any solutions to offer, but I do have a parallel to draw which might give you a slightly different view point on this subject.

I suspect my opinion here might not be widely shared, as it disputes the current view that these people are an exclusively Muslim problem, the like of which we have not previously seen. In fact a closely parallel situation occurred between the years 1936 – 39 during the Spanish civil war. The motivation then was political rather than religious, but that makes no difference; what happened as a result of that motivation is strongly reminiscent of what's happening today.

Several hundred British young men, and it was mainly men, made their way to Spain to join the British Battalion of the International Brigade, to fight on the Republican side against General Franco's Nationalists and his German and Italian allies. You may say that was different, they were fighting fascism, and with the outbreak of the Second World War in 1939 the whole country would soon be fighting fascism. They were just quicker off the mark than their compatriots.

But to say that is to apply the convenient gloss of hindsight, and you should never, ever, forget that treason is a matter of dates. You make your move on this date and they'll give you a medal - make it on that date, and it's a last cigarette and a blindfold.

From contemporary sources the primary motivation of these volunteers seems to have been less concerned with fighting fascism than with supporting communism, and if you want to apply hindsight, then that doesn't look too good with our present awareness of where that led. When you ask if they were they fighting Franco or supporting Stalin, that puts a rather different complexion on things. Stalin killed many times more people than Hitler ever did, so was he really the man to be fighting for?

It is often said that the Condor Legion of the emerging Luftwaffe committed atrocities in Spain, notably in the bombing of Guernica, so surely anyone on the other side of that fight had to be noble and honourable? You may think that, especially when you have Picasso as your in house artist, but only until you take a look at some of the atrocities committed by the Republicans themselves. It is also helpful to bear in mind that the Soviet supplied Republican air force outnumbered the Condor Legion throughout the war, and they were not one whit more choosy about who they bombed or machine gunned, they just had a better publicist.

It was a very nasty and vicious war, with multiple atrocities all round, which is why the bitterness is only just subsiding today. There were no good guys.

The unspeakably vile brutality of the current Islamic State is made more immediately graphic and shocking by being brought to you in your own home on the internet, but the reality of that still hasn't exceeded the brutality, the widespread suffering and the number of deaths in Spain. And right in the middle of this were the British Battalion of the International Brigade; the Number One Company of which was named after the Labour party leader, Clement Atlee, later to become the British Prime Minister.

Were any of the British volunteers involved in massacres? It doesn't seem so, most of that war's secrets have probably now emerged and nothing to implicate British volunteers in anything other than routine engagements has surfaced. But nobody knew that at the time, so perhaps the British government should have barred the participants from returning to the UK, they were after all now trained fighters with allegiance to a foreign cause. Does that sound familiar, from recent newspaper comments?

It might be claimed that the combatants returning from Spain, unlike those returning from Iraq and Syria, had absolutely no interest in creating havoc in their own home country, and that would be true. However, that would be to ignore the fact that they had knowingly and willingly allied themselves to an aggressive foreign power that had every intention of damaging Britain and its interests.

Ample evidence of that is provided by Stalin's mutual non aggression pact with Hitler, the Molotov-Ribbentrop Pact, which sought to distance the Soviet Union from the forthcoming fight for democracy and freedom. Although the Russians ultimately provided the biggest single contribution to winning the fight against Hitler, they only did so after Hitler had double crossed them and launched his massive invasion of Russia. Their preferred option had always been to watch Britain fight the Nazis single handed. How would these returning volunteers have behaved during the war, if Germany had not forced the issue by invading Russia?

If the British government had barred the returning veterans of the Spanish Civil War, who would have been involved? Stephen Spender, the poet; Laurie Lee, the author of Cider With Rosie; Jack Jones, later leader of the biggest union in Britain (and a paid communist agent); Will Paynter, later General Secretary of the National Union of Mineworkers; a nephew of Winston Churchill, an Olympic gold medal winner, a clutch of doctors, and on and on. There were several hundred of them.

Not a single one of these people regarded their involvement in this foreign war with any noticeable embarrassment, in fact most of them regarded it as a badge of honour and dined out on it for the rest of their lives. All you have to do now is to try and work out how that behaviour was so very different from what's going on today.

I would agree there are some differences, but hardly any of these differences reflect favourably on the volunteers. Already in 1936 it was well known, to anyone who didn't have their eyes screwed tight shut and their fingers in their ears, that the communist control of Soviet Russia was much more repressive, murderous and plain nastier than anything the Tsars had ever attempted.

At that time, recent Soviet history included the mass murder of the land owning peasants, known as kulaks, who had been killed by the million during the 1920s (quite literally by the million, a common estimate being seven million), and that was just one of a variety of purges.

This information was widely and authoritatively reported in western newspapers, and on the BBC, and would have been well known to every single one of those young men who so eagerly travelled to Spain to join the International Brigade. A Brigade that was largely equipped by Stalin, and fought to support his aim of exporting communist control to Spain.

The Russians even had a name for such western dupes for their propaganda, they called them *useful idiots*. No matter what anyone tells you: democracy was never even remotely on the menu – from either side.

The most visible contrast between the fighters then and now, seems not to have been the intelligence of the recruits, so much as their maturity. The current crop appear to have less of it, being largely recruited from naive and inadequate individuals, who have usually failed at whatever they have previously attempted. They seem to believe the automatic rifle they're all so desperate to get their hands on will be an extension of their manhood. Their connection to Islam often no more than a cover for juvenile sociopathic urges.

Whereas in the 1930s the stimulus moving most volunteers seems to have been more a collective delusion, than an individual one. A whole stratum of

British society had convinced itself, in the awful shadow of what they called The Great War, that the rise of the right wing dictators was such a threat to world peace that it was worth paying any price to oppose it.

Starting with Mussolini, then Hitler and now, next in line, Franco – where would it end? At first glance this appears to be a much more intellectually respectable position, surely they had a point?

There's no doubt their argument had force, the trouble lay in how they chose to express that opinion. They got into bed with Stalin, a man considerably more murderous than all the other dictators added together, and a man every bit as determined to carve up first Europe, and then the rest of the world, into his own murderous image.

Are the current Islamic State gangsters, and their sick death cult, really murdering more of their prisoners, or doing it more brutally than the combatants in the Spanish Civil War? No they're not, in fact they're not even close to those numbers, the significant point being that in Spain they didn't have the technology to record and then distribute such stomach churning images. Had they possessed it, then I have absolutely no doubts that both sides would have used it.

I don't suggest that the current willingness of some Muslims to butcher either each other, or anyone else they dislike, is a mirror image of the Spanish Civil War, history is a continuous series of echoes, but it rarely repeats itself verbatim. There is an obvious difference in the extent to which the fighting was then confined to one country, but is now so promiscuously dispersed, but apart from that there are a great many similarities.

The depressing fact is that this situation, whereby some of our more viciously feeble minded citizens choose to fight in brutal wars of foreign repression, is a continuation of history, not a departure from it.

That might not be much help in indicating how we should react this time, but it is still useful to remember this isn't the first time we've been here.

CHAPTER EIGHTEEN

Various Random Conclusions
- and God save me from certainty

The last three chapters have been somewhat darker than what came before, and I suppose that's unavoidable if you're going to talk about serious subjects, especially where you're unhappy about some of the things you can see happening around you. In this last section of the book I would like to abandon the wider view and look more personally.

There are some certainties in life, beyond even death and taxes. Never believe anyone who tells you there's a cheque in the post, or who tells you that, 'Ah but this time it will be different'. Never sit on a warm lavatory seat, and never, ever, wear blue socks with brown shoes – are you mad? The sort of lessons in life that you pass onto your children.

But is there anything more substantial than even these weighty nuggets? Yes, there is, but not as much as I used to think. There isn't some whole corpus of esoteric knowledge to be studied for a lifetime and endlessly discussed, there are instead, I would venture to suggest, a few straightforward basics.

I believe in the existence of a supreme being, a creator, even on most days, of the existence of a Christian God. I believe in the existence of the human soul and of a life beyond the one I'm currently living. The usual term would be life after death, but I don't have enough details to be specific. That's the basic stuff, I could probably tidy that list up a little and get it down to less than twenty words. How minimalist do you want to make this?

I have to admit to feeling a bit of a fraud, in having acquired any religious beliefs I possess with the help of the signposts and pointers I described earlier. I would agree that the acquisition of faith without such very large pointers might be more admirable. What I can never know is the extent to which other people experience events of similar significance in their own lives, and the real question between us is; how we interpret our experiences.

But however acquired, I think my membership of a religion, in my case the Church of England, provides a means for me to approach God. It provides a framework in which my beliefs can operate and relate to the rest of my life, a bridge between me and the unknown.

My relationship with an identifiable face of God, and there has to be some identity, if only for my own imagination to work, is with the biblical figure of Jesus. It is most specifically not with the more abstract notion of Father, Son and Holy Spirit. I hope I don't get drummed out for saying this, but not only do I not understand that concept, but I have never found it remotely helpful. Visualising God as Jesus, or I suppose any other identifiable figure, allows me to feel there is a human contact with something bigger, more reliable and simply better than me. It gives me somebody up there to talk to.

I know I'm repeating this point from earlier, but it seems worth it. At my father's funeral I was shocked by how such a loud, forceful and emotionally big man could possibly be fitted into such a small coffin. My sense of loss was not so much for his presence in my life, he had been ill and not himself for some time before his death, but for the loss of someone above me as it were. He hadn't controlled or supervised my life in any way for years, but had still in some way been the senior figure in that life, and now suddenly he was gone, and now *I* was the senior figure. I had become my father. I claim no copyright on this experience, it must have been shared by millions, it's just that it only matters when it hits you personally.

My point is that I think my relationship with God is like that, a senior figure who doesn't interfere in my daily life, but whose very existence provides a backstop for reference and comparison. The person from whom my moral compass derives and, in case of doubt or conflict, the person to whom reference can be made. Perhaps to a blasphemous extent, there is a distinct lack of reverence in this interaction with what I regard as an everyday presence in my life.

Returning to my description of my school days, I would describe the relationship as 'robust'. With comments such as, 'That's another fine mess you've got me into.' sometimes flitting across my mind.

I have never imagined a God of special times or places, and I wouldn't think that I was any more likely to encounter God in church on Sunday, than in the gun shop on Monday. If God exists at all, then some essential part of him is a part of all of us, one more of those bits that you won't find at a post mortem, no matter how determinedly detailed your dissection.

I could say that I imagine God standing beside me at certain times, and asking if some course of action or other was such a good idea. The trouble is that although that's true, it makes God sound like no more than the embodiment of my conscience, and there's more to it than that. I accept that this almost filial relationship is an imagined construct of my own making, without the slightest concrete or even scriptural backing, and that doesn't bother me in the slightest. I find it personally helpful to have God expressed in everyday terms, I'm afraid that you'll have to make your own arrangements.

If you're interested in reading an account of a fictional person with similar views on their relationship to God, you could try one of the Merrily Watkins books by a writer called Phil Rickman. I'm not his agent, his publicist or even his brother in law, I just enjoy the books, and his lead character expresses a range of views that could often have come from me.

When it comes to churchgoing, I go for the reasons outlined earlier in this book, some religious, some not. The primary spiritual reasons for my attendance being to receive Holy Communion and for private prayer.

The Communion service offers what the church calls forgiveness of sins, or redemption, for which I'm grateful, but my own strongest impression of its effect is that it provides a separation from a different time. It draws a line. The past is a foreign country, they do things differently there – I did, but now I've moved on. Holy Communion permits that in a way that nothing else I've ever encountered comes close to.

Freudian analysis cannot achieve in twenty years what the Communion service manages in twenty minutes; usually in better surroundings and set to music. In fact Freudian analysis may be fairly regarded as the rich and gullible person's version of

Communion, it's just a pity it doesn't work. Besides which I couldn't take it myself, my toilet training was wholly without incident and I never fancied my mother.

Medical researchers have been talking for years about the chemical basis of human behaviour, moving seamlessly from the anti depressant to the anti malicious pill. Perhaps there will, one day, be a pill to cure evil, but would you trust it? And would it be such a good idea, for humanity to live subject to the whims of medical or judicial fashion?

Think back to what was done to Alan Turing, the Enigma Code breaker, in the 1950s. In order to avoid prison, following a conviction for homosexual activity, he agreed to receive massive doses of oestrogen, the so called chemical castration then thought to 'cure' homosexuality. This caused such devastation to his mind and body that he killed himself, a medical and legal triumph.

Not long before that, the fashion had been to offer similar 'cures' for a variety of mental illnesses by shoving a chisel into the frontal lobes of sufferer's brains, a procedure known as a lobotomy. (I'm not making that bit up about the chisel, some of these procedures were even known as Ice Pick Lobotomies, for horrifyingly obvious reasons.) All this was done by highly qualified doctors, the toast of their profession, in modern well run hospitals in the middle of the twentieth century.

One unfortunate recipient of a lobotomy was the future President Kennedy's younger sister, Rosemary. Following some youthful misbehaviour, considerably less troublesome and offensive than my own, she was forcibly lobotomised; after which she was bed bound, never spoke again and was doubly incontinent for the rest of her life. Yet another medical and legal triumph.

'Ah but that was then, we're so much cleverer now - this time it will be different.' Yeah right, and pigs might fly. It rather seems that if you wish to be moral, rather than immoral, then you're just going to have to do it yourself.

Moving back to what I was saying about church attendance. Not quite so intense, but for me almost as important, is the sense of community and common purpose in a building more sanctified by a thousand years of common usage, than by any consecration by a busload of bishops. The Catholic and Anglican litanies are very similar and serve the same purpose, so I don't even think that the changeover of the Reformation detracts from its history.

I usually enjoy the rest of the service in different ways and for different reasons. Partly for the period of meditative calm it offers in a busy world, and also for the readings, the hymns and yes, even the sermons. These individual things can be pleasurable and thought provoking, or sometimes even boring, but for me they're still secondary to the Communion and the private prayer.

In the same way that I'm prepared to use the period in church before the service to practise my mind calming routine, so I'm also happy to use time outside church for reading Saint Paul's letters, or other books about religion. I don't see any barriers between the two parts of my life, in fact I don't even see them as separate parts, it's just one life - lived as best I can. But then exploring religion outside of church is what we're both doing now; me by writing this, and you by reading it.

Anyway, you don't have to look too far back to see that church services never used to be as solemn, or as formal, as they sometimes can be now. Try reading

Pepys' Diaries and see what he was thinking about during the sermon. Medieval churches were also marketplaces and community halls, they were normally the only big enclosed public building in the area. In times of war or civil unrest they were frequently used for stabling horses.

Until the introduction of fixed pews in the sixteenth century, the only church seats for the bulk of the congregation were a few wooden benches. But, as with the lifeboats on the Titanic, there were never enough to go round, so most people stood.

This meant that even during services, particularly in the larger churches, there would be a constant background of chatter and movement. Eating and drinking during the services was relatively common. It was the introduction of fixed pews which, very literally, put everyone in their place. That's why some pews, usually at the front, were reserved; they were reserved for the people who'd paid for them.

This must have called for a very different type of preaching. If you're faced with rows of neatly organised modern parishioners sat in straight rows on fixed seats, all looking in your direction rather than talking to each other, you might be able to manage a quiet and reasoned sermon. You might take them through your various carefully detailed points and even hope that one or two of them will follow your reasoning. But if you were faced with a church full of people all on their feet, shuffling around, facing in different directions, eating pies and talking to each other, then you've got a much bigger challenge.

During and after the Second World War in London there was a popular establishment in Soho called the Windmill Theatre. It was the only place in the country licensed by the Lord Chamberlain in which fully naked

271

women could appear on stage, the only proviso was that they weren't allowed to move. If they stood still they were regarded as classical statues and it was art, but if they jiggled their bits about, it was pornography. They had comedians appearing between the nude acts, and those comedy slots were said to be the toughest booking in show business, worse even than the Glasgow Empire. Whatever the punters had turned up for, it wasn't the jokes. I imagine preaching in some medieval churches must have been a similarly uphill struggle.

Another noticeable difference would have been the bright colours that most church interiors were painted, not just the murals of biblical scenes, but the walls and timber beams and even the roof panels would often be coloured. The current restrained mixture of plain grey stone, white plaster and brown wood is a modern idea, and not necessarily an improvement. And it wasn't just the colours, church was where you went to hear music, the latest music and the best music.

Until the eighteenth century the greater proportion of all music was religious music, and this wasn't solely because the composers were especially reverent. The fact is that before the advent of publically available concert halls, the only place in which to perform in public was very often in a church. Not unnaturally the churches expected that the music played in their buildings should have a religious purpose, for example a mass, or a requiem mass.

Furthermore, as there was hardly ever any means of making people pay to hear the music, the churches didn't charge their congregations, the only alternative was that people had to be paid to actually write the music. Hence the fierce competition for appointments such as cathedral choir master or organist, or to be the Master of Music in a royal household.

I can see that I'm starting to get carried away about churches, you could almost think I was preaching to you, but just before I move on, there is one more aspect of the church's role in the community.

Beyond the religion, the meeting place, the poetry, the painting and the music there was also the wood carving. The rood screen, between the chancel, where the altar is, and the main body of the church, was often the most richly decorated part of the building. That, and the ornamental wooden font covers could be intricate and beautiful works of art in their own right, completing the list of what were probably the only works of art that most of the population would ever see.

True, there were lots of grubby dirty little churches, with grubby dirty little incumbents, but there were also some of the crowning glories of the greatest artists and architects of the day, freely on offer to anyone who cared to look. Until, of course, Cromwell knocked them about a bit, but by that time art was becoming more widely available anyway.

I know that I go on about this sort of thing too much, and that it's only some dusty old wooden carvings, but if you live in Britain then you need go no further than St. Paul's Cathedral in London, where the Grinling Gibbons carvings on the choir stalls will assuredly knock your socks off.

*****

I previously expressed some sceptical thoughts on the purity of charity, which were not perhaps the mainstream view on that subject. My opinions on making money might be similarly at odds with the current received wisdom. I don't share Gordon Gekko's conviction that greed is good, but that is still closer to the truth than is sometimes comfortable to acknowledge. Doctor Johnson phrased the sentiment more elegantly, 'There are few ways in which a man can be more innocently employed than in getting money'.

Doctors are trained to disbelieve their patient's estimates of the amounts they eat, drink and smoke, usually doubling any figure they're given. I disbelieve anyone who claims their actions are motivated by charity. We all disbelieve the compensation seeking litigant who claims their case is not just about the money. (Yes it is, yes it is, yes it is.) And as for people's claims of their sexual activity . . . So who *do* I believe? How about the man or woman who claims, or more often shamefacedly admits, to working all hours of day and night in their own business, and hopes thereby to make a fortune? That I believe, and hope they succeed.

Commerce is neither vulgar nor selfish, it is essential. It is the only means yet discovered to provide the funds required to pay for the public services we all so unthinkingly expect. What is truly selfish is the person unwilling to get their own hands dirty, metaphorically or literally, who wishes to hold themselves above such menial details, in the expectation that someone else will do all the donkey work for them.

You might not care to hear this, but running an Oxfam shop is in no more ethical or honourable an occupation than running a gun shop, and I've done both. In fact it may be safely allowed that the unending requirement of any commercial organisation to pay its bills introduces a degree of reality that the public sector and the charity shop will always lack.

A commercial company cannot draw its funds from the public purse, or have some minister argue for an increase in the Chancellor's next spending round, it has to go into the market place and actually *make* any money it wants to spend. The company that doesn't pay its wages goes to the wall. One occasionally feels this tedious detail has escaped the attention of some clergymen and politicians.

Providing employment to yourself and others, paying your taxes and paying your own way in life, might sound rather dull and worthy and it will never qualify you to receive a medal, nor should it, but it is an essentially honest and decent life style. There is nothing wrong with being a teacher or a nurse, these are worthwhile, honourable and necessary callings, but public sector occupations are not the sole repositories of virtue. Some grubby oik in the background has to pay for them, and to do so without the benefit of any claim to moral superiority.

A recurrent claim of a certain type of person working in the public sector, sometimes even made with a straight face, is that they would, *of course*, have made much more money in the private sector. The implication is that they have nobly and selflessly devoted their lives to the public good. Apart from demonstrating a deep and profound ignorance of the private sector, this takes us neatly back to my opinion of those who claim to be motivated by nothing but charity.

Any use of that self indulgent phrase, 'The caring professions' tells you a lot more about the unfocussed myopia of the person using it, than the nature of the so called profession. Greed might not be good, but honest, money making commerce most certainly is.

*****

I now find myself in my late sixties, contemplating retirement and, if I live long enough, impending old age, do I have any summary of my beliefs? Not exactly a summary, in the sense of something neat and packaged. I've said what I feel about religion and God, I've moaned about the Church of England's inability to say anything coherent about abortion or euthanasia, and I've moaned about the unwillingness of some Muslims to integrate more fully, so what's left?

Old age is supposed to be a shipwreck, and maybe it will be when I get there, but already some things that have always been there can be seen and understood more clearly now, than when younger. You don't get any smarter as you get older, if you keep your wits about you then you'll learn some new things and new tricks, but knowledge isn't wisdom. It just sometimes looks like it when you recycle the lessons learned from old experiences.

I don't want to find myself engaged in that annoying and patronising trait you sometimes encounter, whereby rich people deliver uncalled for lectures about how unimportant money is to them. Sadly I'm not rich enough to do that, although I think I'd quite enjoy it if I were. Even so it is true that the acquisition of mere *things* becomes less important than before, while the quality and importance of the things you do have becomes much more relevant. Quality becomes more important than quantity, but then I would say that having just moved from a rambling seven bedroom house to a compact three bedroom house.

I'm at an age where I need to identify and concentrate on those things essential to this stage of life, rather than clinging to those things that used to be important - that's one of the aspects of downsizing: dumping stuff is quite liberating.

One of the things I can see more clearly now, is not that I was ever wrong to worry about the BBC, but that I no longer need do so quite so keenly. By the BBC I refer to the sort of things we all worry about when lying awake at three o'clock in the morning, you can take your pick from those three circling black crows in the night: Betrayal, Bankruptcy and Cancer.

To run through those possibilities in order: I have by now experienced betrayal (but not by my wife or children), and learnt that the Devil is not some creature with horns and a forked tail, if only it were that easy. Unhappily, the Devil is someone you know well, someone you would open the door to late at night, someone you trust completely, perhaps even someone you love; no one else is close enough to wound.

Although never having been bankrupt, I have viewed that possibility from frighteningly close quarters, and Margaret and I have both had cancer. I would never want to be cocky about my abilities to cope with life's slings and arrows, but I'm beginning to get the feeling that even if I can't cope with whatever it is that turns up next, I will at least have given it my best shot before finally going under.

Then there's the fact that the things you worry about change as you grow older, at first you think your relationships and your work are all important, at some stage you might even have thought something as stupid as what car you drove was important; but then you have children, and that changes everything, forever. Suddenly someone else's interests are at least as important as your own, and in many cases more so.

Now I notice things I never would have, in this morning's paper there was an article about some supposed injection that would shortly be made available for all, it's claimed to prevent dementia. Despite being well aware that all such forthcoming miracle drug stories turn out to be hooey, I still found myself wondering – will that be ready in time for me? I was gullible when I was young, then I got a little smarter for a while, and now I'm getting gullible all over again.

When it comes to my final years, I have some good news waiting for me. I came into this world on a 26th. of February, a completely unremarkable fact until you know that I should have arrived in the first week of that month. I was over two and a half weeks late and weighed eleven pounds twelve ounces, and to overcome my reluctance to emerge naturally, had to be dragged out with forceps. This has left a permanent scar down the right side of my neck, I've just put my fingers into it now, and that was the cause of me being paralysed down the left side of my body for the first twelve months of my life.

The doctor who delivered me, an old army friend of my father's from the war, who was probably better with gunshot wounds than babies, told me all about this when I was old enough to understand, and then added an extra snippet. He said that it was often the case that babies paralysed in this way during their earliest years, would encounter the same problem in their final years.

'So I'm going to be paralysed for the last year of my life?'

'Well obviously not, if you're run over by a bus or something first, you stupid boy, but otherwise, probably yes.'

'Oh, that's nice to know, thank you doctor.'

I have never bothered to check on the reliability of this prognosis as I don't imagine there's a lot to be done about it. But if it is true, then unlike the rest of you, at least I'll get a twelve month warning, in which to spend all my money and behave disgracefully – if a little stiffly.

My final thoughts on this subject are not to emphasise my belief in God, but rather to highlight my belief in the benefit of doubts and questions. God save me from certainty, that final slamming shut of the mind's door. A sliver of doubt and uncertainty is like putting salt on your food, it makes you appreciate what you have all the more.

#####

Other books by Ian Okell,
all works of fiction,
which might or might not be
to your taste, are listed in the
following pages. They are shown
in order of their original publication.

Loose Cannon

Ian Okell

Harry Lyndon is a civilised and happy man, his world organised just the way he likes it. But then, out of the blue, someone tries to kill him - and he has no idea who or why.

The trouble is that when he tells the police it turns out they also want him dead. Something is horribly wrong, He's forced to run, with nothing but the clothes on his back. It isn't mistaken identity. His credit cards have been cancelled, his flat watched and his girlfriend disappeared. He is the named subject of a full scale terrorist alert - and they're going to shoot him on sight.

Only one thing might help - without his anti psychotic tablets he's getting more than a little unstable himself - dangerously so. Somebody, somewhere, thought he'd be a pushover . . .

'It isn't paranoid to think they're trying to kill you - not if it's true. Loose Cannon takes up where The 39 Steps and Rogue Male left off.'

Published by - feedaread.com

Rude Awakening

Ian Okell

"They were either going to install me as the Arch Druid, or they had something of a sacrificial nature in mind. Perhaps I should tell them I wasn't a virgin."

He already knew his cancer was terminal and lying in hospital, finally surrendering to the morphine, Michael accepts that he is dying. But suddenly it's all gone wrong - he's awake when he should be dead, and in a place he's never seen before.

Is this just the random sparking of failing brain cells before the last goodbye? Is this what death feels like? Out of place and out of time - even realising that he is still alive doesn't do him any good. He is at the wrong end of an impossible journey, in a society untouched by civilisation.

'Tangled and dangerous relationships in a sweeping saga of conflict, betrayal and discovery. As seen through the eyes of an entertaining and extremely devious observer.'

Published by - feedaread.com

Charlie Chaplin's Uncle

Ian Okell

London, December 1892 – A mist drifts in from the river – on the streets there are gas lamps and Hansom cabs. There are dirty doings at the music hall and even dirtier doings on the Royal Train.

The Prince of Wales has designs on another man's wife and visiting Royalty look like getting shot – one way or another somebody is going to come to a sticky, sticky end.

The Freemasons are in there somewhere, but what's their interest? Then things really begin to fall apart. The constabulary turn out to be no use at all – and meanwhile the body count is rising – inexorably.

Who's going to be the most help: young Charlie Chaplin, Sherlock Holmes, or Mr. Fowler the engine driver?

'A Victorian railway caper in a snowstorm, gripping, ruthless, and very funny.
An absolutely brilliant book, fantastic fun. Just read it!'

Published by - feedaread.com

Rendezvous in Paris

Ian Okell

France, May 1940. The German Blitzkrieg thrusts deep into France – the French army is on the point of collapse. Amid the confusion a British Military Intelligence mission team are sent to snatch a missing radar part.

It's a disaster: and the team's sole survivor, retired scientist Sir Freddy Villiers, is ordered home. But he reckons there's still a chance, and with help from alluring female Gendarme Martine Dumont, he could be right.

Unfortunately, German agent Heidi Fuchs has other ideas. She's cunning, she's dirty and she's utterly ruthless. Freddy's out of his league. But the fortunes of war are never straightforward and it seems there's more at stake than radar.

While the battle for France rages unchecked, the hunt gets increasingly personal, the emotions more confused, and Sir Freddy needs to answer one very basic question: Which comes first – the mission or Martine?

'Heidi – one of fiction's more engaging psychopaths, a great book – nail biting to the very last page. A top writer on top form.'

Published by – feedaread.com

Barabbas

Ian Okell
(Writing as **Ian Lindsay**)

Jerusalem AD 33 – A city in uproar, the authorities struggle to keep the peace.

A surprisingly candid view of the turmoil that followed the death of Jesus, as reported by the luckiest man in the city, the unrepentant crook Barabbas. Offered assistance by Jesus' friends, who see him as a suitable case for charity, he sees himself as being more in need of hard cash and quick way out of town.

This account of his reluctant but deepening involvement with the central figures of the early church shows the shocked and frightened disciples, the men and women who would later be called saints, in a less than flattering, but very human light.

The struggle for leadership throws up a surprising winner, a man at odds with Peter, a man reluctant to accept either women in authority or Gentiles into the faith. Through all this, and the growing emergence of Paul, moves the overshadowed but watchful figure of Barabbas, still unsure of his own beliefs, but reporting everything he sees around him.

'A plausible and fascinating suggestion of what might have happened. Why has no one written this story before?'

Published by – feedaread.com

Dirty

Ian Okell

Set in the present day, in the US, Syria and London.

MI6's agent in Islamic State is running for his life, his cover blown, but desperate to get his information out. While in London, the terrorists finalise their plans for a massive radioactive dirty bomb in the crowded heart of the City.

The components for the bomb are all in place, the Metropolitan Police are doing their best, but it isn't enough. At every turn the bombers are one step ahead, killing anyone who stands in their way – police officers, bystanders and even their own people.

The only opponents the terrorists haven't allowed for are an injured man who should still be in hospital, a mentally unstable jihadi bride bent on revenge, and an MI6 analyst, who despite her skills has never seen active duty. Deep underground there is a desperate game of cat and mouse on the swaying, rattling carriages of the London Tube.

'A fast moving chase with believable characters straight off the evening news, it's been well researched - the technical detail seems uncomfortably possible – and very Dirty.'

Published by feedaread.com

All these books are available either in paperback or e-book download in most standard formats: Kindle, Apple, Sony, Kobo Nook, Smashwords etc. Full details are available on Amazon or any major bookseller's Ian Okell page.

Lightning Source UK Ltd.
Milton Keynes UK
UKOW04f0101110615

253311UK00001B/4/P